Trauma and Teens

A Guide and Toolbox for Working Towards Wellbeing in Schools and Homes

Frédérique Lambrakis-Haddad

Trauma and Teens
A Guide and Toolbox for Working Towards Wellbeing in Schools and Homes

© Pavilion Publishing & Media

The author has asserted her rights in accordance with the Copyright, Designs and Patents Act (1988) to be identified as the author of this work.

Published by:
Pavilion Publishing and Media Ltd
Blue Sky Offices
25 Cecil Pashley Way
Shoreham by Sea
West Sussex
BN43 5FF
UK

Tel: 01273 434 943
Email: info@pavpub.com
Web: www.pavpub.com

Published 2022

All rights reserved. No part of this publication may be reproduced, stored in a retrieval system, or transmitted in any form or by any means, electronic, mechanical, photocopying, recording or otherwise, without the prior permission in writing of the publisher and the copyright owners.

A catalogue record for this book is available from the British Library.

ISBN: 978-1-80388-008-2

Pavilion Publishing and Media is a leading publisher of books, training materials and digital content in mental health, social care and allied fields. Pavilion and its imprints offer must-have knowledge and innovative learning solutions underpinned by sound research and professional values.

Author: Frédérique Lambrakis-Haddad
Editor: Michael Benge, Pavilion Publishing and Media
Cover design: Emma Dawe, Pavilion Publishing and Media
Page layout and typesetting: Emma Dawe, Pavilion Publishing and Media
Printing: CMP Digital Print Solutions

"This book is an invaluable resource for anyone who parents, cares for or educates teens who are experiencing trauma in any of its forms. It is rich with insight, advice and detail but remains very accessible to any reader. This includes teenagers themselves, allowing them a greater understanding of the situations they are experiencing and their reactions to the challenging world around them.

"Every adult knows that the adolescent years are seldom straightforward, but for some the addition of trauma can make them extremely distressing and confusing – not only for the individual, but also for the teachers and family around them. This book will give the reader a better understanding of the impact of trauma on young lives, guide development of the tools required to achieve more positive outcomes, and ultimately help teenagers to become happier and healthier adults.

"Frédérique covers all aspects of wellbeing for teens – from having better conversations to the impact of sleep and nutrition and the importance of play. I know from personal experience that had this book been available to me as a teen it would have been enormously beneficial when dealing with the challenges I was facing. Any book that helps teenagers move away from self-destructive behaviours connected with shame and guilt and towards better awareness and a happier, less stressful life is a must."

Zoe Lyons
Comedian and Presenter

"Do not be misled by the simplicity of the pen portraits that sketch out the challenges so many of us face as parents and educators. This book is filled with insightful and practical resources that will give you greater confidence in dealing with the complexities that Covid in particular has exacerbated for young people. It will also give you greater self-awareness and appreciation of the qualities you might bring to the table in providing support to whoever you are here to help, and however much they might need you."

Cheryl Giovannoni
Chief Executive, Girls' School Day Trust

"What counts in life is not the mere fact that we have lived. It is what difference we have made to the lives of others that will determine the significance of the life we lead."

Nelson Mandela

This book is dedicated to my seven Pillars of Wellbeing:

My beloved parents, Claude and George, who gave me a secure and such a loving start, present and future.

Jocelyne, whose warmth and gentle care was always by my side growing up.

Alex, my sister, who was my accomplice and friend when navigating our childhood upheavals.

Raph, Sovanne and Lawrence, who are forever my loves, rocks and profound joys.

About the Author

 Frédérique Lambrakis-Haddad is a child and adolescent therapist, the lead practitioner of www.traumainform.com and a co-founder of Brighton and Hove based registered charity for mentoring for young women (including non-binary) called Flourish Mentors (www.flourishmentors.com/). She also has a private practice where she sees young people for therapy and loves every moment she spends with them.

Frédérique has always been passionate about mental health and young people. It was after working with excluded teens in Brighton and Hove for 15 years that she grew inspired to write this book in order to help parents, carers and schools.

Frédérique has worked with adults and young people both in the US and UK for over 30 year. She brings expertise in mental health, extensive experience working with trauma and its effects, but also a deep knowledge and experience of living and working internationally. In addition to Frédérique's personal family and background which are international, she also holds a Master's degree in Clinical Social Work with a mental health specialisation from University of Maryland and a Master's degree from the Fletcher School of Law and Diplomacy, from Tufts University in Boston. More recently, she completed a two year post-graduate psychotherapy course at the Tavistock and Portman Clinic in London, UK. In the US and the UK, she worked in mental health clinics and residential centres specialising in working with young people and adults who had experienced significant sexual, emotional and physical abuse and neglect. She also has recently completed a Coaching and Mentoring diploma with College of Management and IT (CMIT).

Frédérique is a passionate and tenacious advocate for young peoples' emotional and mental health needs at the centre of interventions and thinking. Always.

Contents

About the Author vii

Introduction 1

Part 1 Case studies of teen trauma 9

    Chapter 1: Bullying 11

    Chapter 2: Cyberbullying 17

    Chapter 3: Parental abuse and neglect 23

    Chapter 4: Identity issues 27

    Chapter 5: Body image disorder 33

    Chapter 6: The trauma of (undiagnosed) mental health issues 37

    Chapter 7: Social isolation 43

    Chapter 8: Divorce 47

    Chapter 9: Loss of a loved one 51

    Chapter 10: Fostering and adoption 57

Part 2 Useful ideas and concepts 63

    Chapter 11: Grief and loss 65

    Chapter 12: Attachment theory and styles 73

    Chapter 13: Trauma and our bodies 87

Part 3 Trauma Toolbox 93

    Chapter 14: Working with PACE 95

    Chapter 15: Self-regulation and grounding techniques 99

    Chapter 16: The importance of self-care 103

    Chapter 17: Key strategies for parents and carers 111

    Chapter 18: Key strategies for teachers and other educators 115

    Chapter 19: Resources 119

Introduction

To give you a taste of what is to come, let me introduce you to Zoe.

Zoe's story

"I don't sleep well and I have lots of nightmares. The only way I can get to sleep is to smoke weed. I can't tell anyone about the nightmares. Mum and Dad will be mad and they'll figure it out. They've told me a million times to wait until I'm in love. My friends won't understand. I'm such an idiot. I know my skirt was too short; but he was so cute! And I felt special. He asked me to walk with him in the park, but then he wouldn't stop kissing me and touching me. I couldn't stop him. It was my first time, I told him no, but he did it anyway. I know it's my fault."

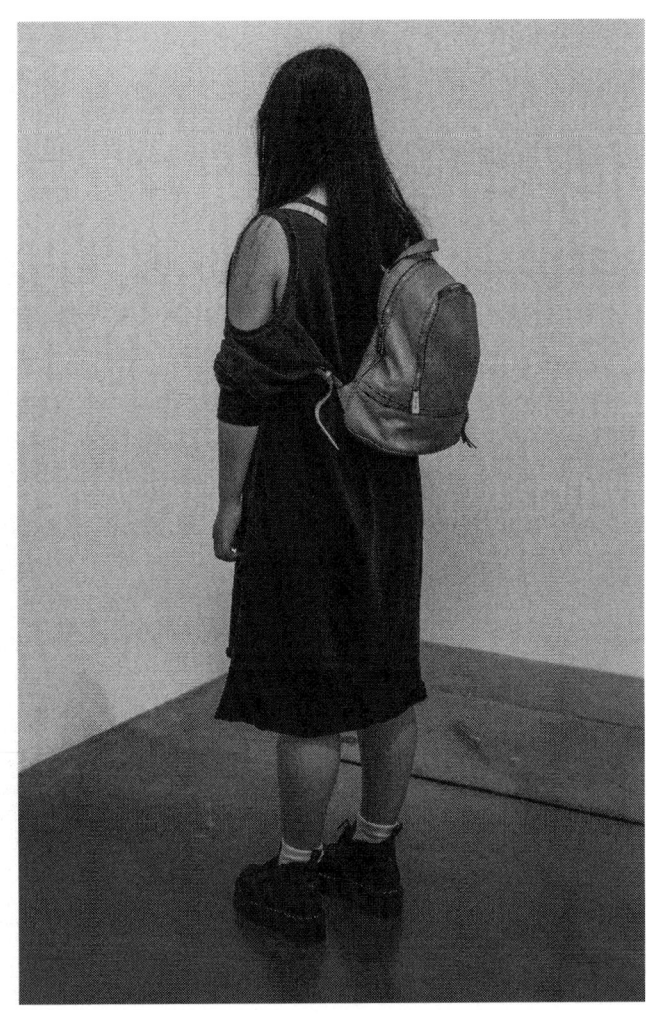

Home worries

"Why is Zoe so different lately? I used to be able to sit down with her and think and discuss things with her, but now she is blocking me out. Her best friend, Elise, does not seem to be calling much anymore and she doesn't seem to go out much. Every time I ask her what is wrong, she blanks me. Is this Zoe becoming the dreaded adolescent she has never been? But my sense is that something else is going on. She looks so sad sometimes but she won't let me in!"

School's viewpoint

"Zoe, 14 years old, lives with her parents in a middle-class home with lots of support and communication – or so it seems. She is pretty, well liked and a good student. Recently Zoe seems to be hanging out with a new group of girls, not her usual group. She has started skipping my class and not turning in school assignments on time, or at all. When I ask her what is going on, she is snide with me. The other day I asked her what she was doing and she snorted: 'Nothing, Miss, you are just so *boring*!' and walked off! All of this in front of her new pals and avoiding eye contact. I did note a slight glaze in her eyes and I wonder whether perhaps she was high. If so, that is new for her."

Zoe's trauma

Zoe is struggling with probable PTSD and feelings of shame, guilt and isolation. Her usual support system feels unavailable to her due to these feelings. One clue is the sudden and significant change in behaviour and her lack of using her usual supports. Her friends and parents were usually people she talked to, but now she is not doing this.

It is easy to personalise and get distracted by Zoe's behaviour, as she may be more disruptive than before, and it may be tempting to give her 'consequences' to keep her from straying onto the 'wrong path'. Her lack of work and new-found boldness towards teachers and her ignoring her parents and friends may feel defiant but it is not.

What Zoe needs is for someone to look at what *underlies* her behaviour, and that is what this book is about. We are going to look at what young people are communicating to us and try not to follow the distractions, but rather follow the clues and uncover what messages they are communicating to us, underneath all the bravado and distracting behaviours.

 CAUTION: PROCEED WITH THOUGHT AND CURIOSITY

"All behaviour (truly) is communication."

You've probably heard this phrase a million times before, but what does it really mean? This book is going to explore how we can look at our teens and become better-equipped parents, carers and educators when they are faced with trauma.

And trauma can be disguised in many forms, so I hope this book will help you uncover it.

Think of yourself as a detective, but with a spirit of genuine curiosity and non-judgment. Try to unpick what underlies the troublesome behaviours your teen might be exhibiting. Your role can shift from being an enforcer of rules to an empathic detective and translator. This book will help you achieve this difficult balance.

The book uses case studies of fictionalized adolescents, like Zoe's story, to explore different traumas. These case studies draw on my 25 years of therapy experience working with adolescents who present with different traumas. I encourage you to share these stories with your teens, as the principle of universality says that we all derive a great deal of comfort from the knowledge that we are not alone in our feelings and despair. You might assume, as an adult, that an adolescent will realize their experience is not isolated. Often, they do not. Their feelings of shame, guilt, pain and anguish isolate many of them. Not only will your teen derive comfort from knowing they are not alone, but there is a curative element, too!

Introduction

In addition to exploring the traumas, our worries and interventions, we will explore other concepts and instruments which can better equip you to work thoughtfully, with creativity and care.

> **Discussion point**
>
> You will find these discussion points scattered throughout this book. They are just that. I invite you to have a think, discuss with your teens, your family and your colleagues some of the suggested points and questions. This book can serve as a springboard for conversation with the adolescents around you. You might be surprised at how insightful, curious and enthusiastic teens get when they hear other young people's stories.

Self-awareness is key to any intervention with teens. The more self-aware you are, the better equipped you will be.

This book hopes to be a pragmatic and interesting toolbox of ideas and interventions which you can easily apply to your traumatised teen.

My tone is conversational and straight shooting; in other words: 'plainspeak'.

So, just a little bit about trauma and trauma types

There are basically four 'types' of trauma. Is it important to know the different types?

Yes and no.

Yes, because it is important to know the range of experiences (which might not have occurred to you before) that might signify a 'traumatic' experience. You might find you did not realize that some of these experiences are legitimately trauma, but they are! You may think of trauma as an earthquake, terrorism or an assault. It is all these things but it is also any event, or series of events, that overwhelms a person's capacity to cope, with a long-lasting impact on that person.

On the other hand the answer is no, because traumas often 'overlap', and though it is important to recognize that the young person has experienced a form/forms of trauma, it does not really matter which kind.

Four trauma types

Acute: Like watching a car crash in front of your eyes, or a single event which causes you great distress, like a rape or the loss of someone you really love. Zoe, who we introduced in our prologue, would fall into this category.

Chronic: Multiple events taking place over time, like living in a war-torn area or living in a home with an alcoholic parent or domestic violence.

Complex: This can often overlap with chronic trauma (and they are often confused, but for our purposes, let's not worry about this now). This type of trauma is prolonged and multiple, like experiencing abuse and neglect in your childhood. I suppose what marks this as different from chronic trauma lies in the word: 'complex' meaning 'multi-layered'. It is about a young person who lives with an abusive parent, who also sees the other parent beaten up and lives in poverty. There are lots of layers to their trauma. Children in care have pretty much all experienced this level of trauma.

Historical and racial transgenerational/intergenerational trauma: This is the most recently recognized category of trauma and, to be honest, a lot of people had not thought of it before the Black Lives Matter (BLM) movement happened. At least not as a form of trauma. This category of trauma includes lots of big words. Perhaps breaking it down might help.

'Historical and racial transgenerational trauma' refers to the psychological and emotional wounding across generations from massive group trauma. Examples of this include colonialism, the transatlantic slave trade, genocides across the world and the Holocaust. This trauma includes the racism which is often the root cause but has lingering effects well after the historic traumatic event has ended. These effects are then carried from generation to generation and create deep, long-term wounds in families and communities.

'Intergenerational trauma' is the trauma transferred between generations. This can include the historic and racial trauma mentioned above, but it can also be extreme poverty, a sudden or violent death of a family member, a crime against a family, a parent who fought in a war, or was a hostage or prisoner of war. Those sorts of impactful life events transform not only the life of the person affected but those around them for generations to come.

A tangible example of this category might be if you have had a great-grandfather who, let's say, was a slave or a prisoner of war. He would have had to numb his emotions to deal with the physical and mental pain and distress he faced daily. His children would therefore have had either an absent father or an emotionally unavailable one.

One can imagine that this emotional disconnection could then easily be passed down from generation to generation. Not because people want to be emotionally unavailable, but because they have not learned anything different. We tend to repeat the parenting models of our own parents or caregivers without questioning them. What we do know about parenting and about attachment (which will be explored in the second half of the book more deeply) is that if you have a carer who is emotionally unavailable as an infant, there will be an insecure pattern of attachment for that young person. This pattern then can be replicated, not with intent, but due to the traumatic origin for generation after generation. It becomes a legacy of trauma.

> **Discussion point**
>
> So, take a minute now and think: have you ever experienced any of these types of traumas? My guess is yes.
>
> Were your traumas recognized?
>
> If so, was it enough to help you get better?
>
> If not, what would have helped?

We are now going to explore different traumas through mini case studies. Most of the cases are loosely based on clients I have worked with in the past. There is a mix of socio-economic classes, stressors and contexts. I have focused on adolescents aged between 11-18 years. I purposely started at 11 years as the British system of education includes 11 year olds in their secondary schools and thereby includes them with other adolescents.

You might find that you, or a teen you know, share similarities with the case studies. This is helpful. Look at what might help them (and you). This list will not be exhaustive, but it focuses on a lot of 'common' traumas young people face today. The good news is that there is a fair amount of overlap and this book aims to shift the approach you might take, which should allow you to tackle what may have felt insurmountable before.

But before we move on, what do we do for Zoe?

Once we recognise that Zoe is traumatised and not just 'acting out', we can respond to her immediately. We can help her to reconnect with her previously existing support systems which are probably still available to her but which she may need help to access. So, how do we do that?

Interventions

Home

If you are Zoe's parent, sit down and chat to her. You may get a lot of resistance, but rather than falling into the trap of arguing and forcing Zoe to talk, create a space where she knows she can talk to you. Give her time. Push away that feeling of urgency and help her to understand, with gentle reminders, that you are there for her and you will accept her whatever she has done. Make sure you tell her that whatever the problem, you will help her unpick it alongside her. You will likely need to persist and expect her to resist, for a while. That is okay you need to follow her pace.

Zoe is likely to feel totally overwhelmed by her problem, so she might just show emotions (crying, low mood, anger) rather than accessing her feelings in a 'reasonable' way, so remember this is *not about you*, but your role as a parent. Your role, in this instance, is to accompany your adolescent and hold her hand, but also to let it go sometimes. An important shift to note here is that one difference between adolescence and earlier childhood is that you should shift your efforts to work 'alongside' rather than 'for' her. This shift in power is subtle, as you may still be the more worldly and knowledgeable one, but she is your partner rather than your 'subject', so to speak.

If you discover that she is using drugs, rather than forbid it and give her 'consequences', unpick with her the reasons why she has started. How much peer pressure is she feeling? Is she using weed to calm down, for example? Does she know what she feels right before she wants to use it? Can she go to sleep without it?

Once you can talk openly about any drug use, then you can start looking at alternatives for her. Replace the weed with something else, for example. We all need a substitute for our poor behaviours. Mindfulness or breathing apps on phones, bedtime rituals and soothing music can all be options (which will be later discussed in Part 3 of this book, called: Trauma Toolbox).

Explore options with her. Build in some playfulness when trying out the options as there might be some degree of trial and error. Some of your ideas will fail, so plan that with her but encourage her to try more helpful coping strategies than weed. All of these can help her learn healthier ways to manage her anxiety and inability to sleep due to worries. It may not be a quick fix, depending on how long the drug use has been going on, but what she is doing is opening up communication with you and that is invaluable.

School

If you are an educator, it is easy to misinterpret Zoe's defiance as 'acting out' behaviours that need consequences. These behaviours are a departure from her norm and this should provide you with a big clue. Marked change in behaviours usually signal that something is amiss, and this is when we need to become detectives and look for what problems underlie this change. Reach out to her.

Give Zoe opportunities to access you without her peers being present, in private, and most importantly allow her a way to save face in front of her peers. So many battles are lost by educators who fall into the trap of listening to teens, literally. Swear words and defiance are simply used to mask an underlying problem. Persist. A young person like Zoe should be relatively easy to reach as her problematic behaviours are new and still forming. Try to help and encourage her to link up to her previous peer group, and encourage them to approach her. Reach out to her parents and uncover if there is more to the story than you have seen. Most of all, persist and rebuild your relationship to the point it once was. If you never had a positive relationship with her, ask a colleague who has.

So, before we look at other case studies, just a note about hypervigilance and trauma. Everyone who has faced trauma will experience hypervigilance, so it is helpful to you just to bear this is mind when our exploration deepens.

Hypervigilance

Hypervigilance is a response that all trauma survivors experience. Its function is protective and it means being in a 'hyper alert' state. When someone is hypervigilant they are extremely attuned to everything, and I mean EVERYTHING, in their environment. They are constantly reading their environment for clues of danger and they will spend quite a lot of energy trying to anticipate the perceived danger and avoid it. In later chapters we will briefly explore our various responses to threat. For right now, however, just bear in mind that when an adolescent has experienced trauma, as in the case studies that follow, they will likely be in hypervigilant mode whether they are aware of it or not. This expends a lot of emotional and physical energy and also often leads to their misreading social cues.

> **Discussion point**
>
> You might find in our case studies described here that there are overlapping types of trauma. If you think this, you would be right! It might be worth reading a case study and showing it to someone (even your teen) to discuss it and talk about which of these types of trauma each case study might fall into. You might be surprised at the insight our young people can have, and you can also use these case studies to begin a tricky conversation with your teen. Please remember: there are no right or wrong answers; they are all forms of trauma.

Part 1
Case studies of teen trauma

Chapter 1: Bullying

The bullied: Max

Max's story: "I just got into Year 7 and I am feeling overwhelmed. I don't know who my friends are anymore, and the fact I am small as I have not grown yet makes me feel insecure. In Year 6, I had my guy friends and it was chill. Now, half of them of are flirting with girls and I just don't feel like I fit in. Plus, this bigger kid, a year above me, has started to hassle me at break time. He and his mates are saying I am a "gay boy" and push me around. I don't know where to go because all my mates are on the field paying footie, but they bother me there too. No one stands up for me because I think they are afraid they will get picked on too. I worry about walking home alone now. He said something about knowing where I live. I have not told my parents because they will just call the school and then I will be a snitch and that is when the real trouble will start."

Home worries: "Max was excited about going to his school, but he seems a bit more distant now. The first year of secondary school is a big change. I guess it might just be teenager stuff or the transition. When I asked him about it the other day, he blew up at me and told me to mind my own business. I just don't know how to reach him anymore.

I feel something is off, but I am not sure what. I could call the school, but I have not even met his form tutor and now that I no longer pick him up at school, like in primary school, I feel disconnected from his friends and their parents."

School's viewpoint: "Max, 12 years old, is living at home with his parents and I don't know much more than that as he is a new Year 7. He seems quite reserved in class and does not participate much. The other day I saw him walk into class with red eyes. I wondered if he had been crying. Come to think of it, I don't see him with the same group of friends around school as he is often on his own. Maybe I need to keep an eye on him?"

Max's trauma: Max is being bullied. Transition year from primary to secondary school is a particularly vulnerable year for young people. Although 12 years old is not technically a teenager, they are immersed in the adolescent school world. Transition into sixth form can also be tricky for similar reasons: it can be very destabilizing to lose the reassurance provided by the familiar school environment with friends, teachers, teaching assistants and the school surroundings with its expectations and routines.

The problem here for Max is not only that is he experiencing the trauma of the bullying, but he is also experiencing the trauma of losing the security that was provided by all which was previously familiar. In other words, in response to being bullied he will try and fall back on his tried and trusted supports of the past. These supports, however, have either disappeared or have been significantly reduced. The sense of loss this presents, and the feeling of disempowerment, can be overwhelming.

Interventions

Home: Max's parents are not aware of the bullying. However, as his parents they need to take on the natural, protective role they have taken with him in the past, while at the same time helping him engage with new transitions and change with a positive and open attitude. Parents often feel quite lost at the beginning of a transition, as their 'familiar' is also lost. But if you have had a good relationship with your son, trust your instincts! Also remember that Year 7 is difficult for many young people.

Once Max's parents do find out that he is being bullied, the difficulty has just begun. If you overprotect a young person, then the bullying will likely increase. Young people who are bullied have generally internalized a victim mentality, and unfortunately bullies can sniff this out and will only exacerbate the bullying if adult protection is detected. The key is for Max to develop more confidence in his ability to express himself with peers and adults. It is a balance of developing his ability to express himself to others with respectful but firm words, body language and tone of voice, even under pressure, while also asking for help from the right people.

School: As an educator, you know that there is bullying going on in your setting. It is up to you to detect who the bullies are and who is being bullied. If you see signs, follow them. Once you have identified the bullied, pull them aside and rather than focus on who is bullying them (as they will most likely resist for fear of consequences), focus on skills they can develop to help themselves. The impact of this intervention is two-fold. First, the child may learn some strategies which will empower them, but it also builds trust in your relationship with them. You may get information without pressuring them, as the last thing a child who is being bullied needs is one more issue to worry about.

What anti-bullying strategies Max can learn to become more confident?

Sadly, there is no magic bullet and it is a very hard to overcome bullying. I have not heard of one school which has not struggled with this. The message to Max, however, should be that a joined-up approach with adults and himself is what is needed. The message to Max is: "Together we will unite and defeat the bullies".

Here is a possible plan of action for Max:

- **Project an attitude of awareness of your surroundings, calmness, respect and confidence (even if you are not feeling it).** Specifically, this includes holding your head high, sitting with a straight back, walking with purpose and walking with a peaceful expression on your face. Use yourself as a role model and if you can, role-play it (in private) with him. Mess about and make fun of yourself, giving him alternatives about how not to appear to others. For example, curve your back and look miserable and ask him if he would want to pick on you if you looked like that? Playfulness and laughter are huge anti-anxiety interventions! The more play, the better!
- **Strategic avoidance:** Teach Max that leaving an unsafe place quickly but with dignity and ("fake it, till you make it") confidence can signal to others that you are not afraid. The key is not to run but to walk away. Teach him scripted phrases that sound confident but are neutral or friendly in tone, such as: 'Wow, I am late for class, gotta go' or 'See you later!' These scripts might distract the bully and get you out of striking distance. Importantly they do not signal fear.
- **Practice calm, firm and polite language:** Boundaries are being broken when bullied. The practice of neutral and calm tones and language can empower Max.
- **Use your voice to articulate your distress if you are being aggressed:** If being hurt, say loudly 'Stop!' or 'I do not like that!' to catch people's attention. Bullies do not want to be caught. Also, many times staff at schools do not hear what is being said between peers and some of their inaction may be due to lack of knowledge.

Discussion point

Can you remember when you have faced bullying, either as a victim or as a bystander? If you are honest with yourself, what makes it difficult to challenge bullying when you see it? Is there any one thing you might change in your response next time you see it or experience it?

Chapter 1: Bullying

The bully (or is it the bullied?): Sam

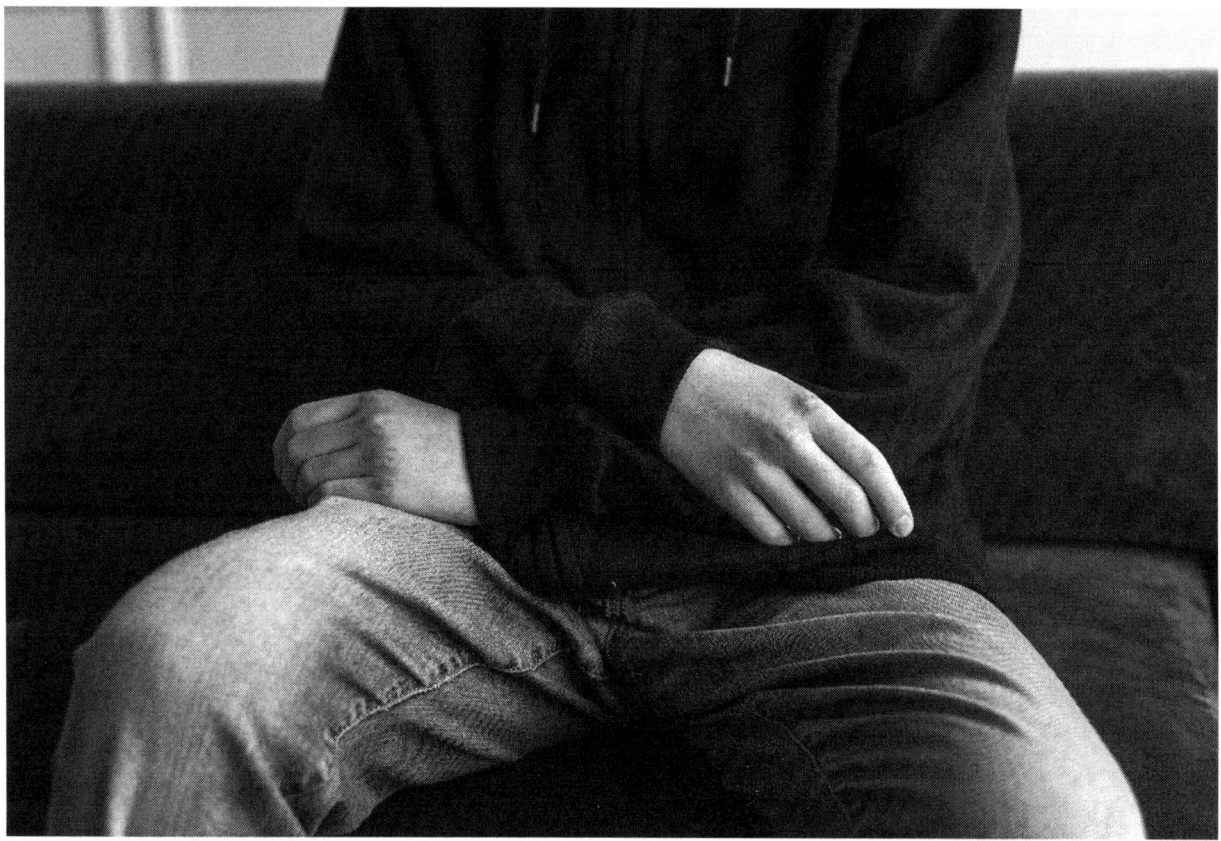

Sam's story. "My mum and sister are my world. Last night mum and dad got into it again. I swear if he hits her again, I am going to kill him. I hate him. He tells me I am a piece of shit, but he is the one who is nasty. I spend a lot of time at the gym and I'm definitely getting cut. One day I will get big enough to kick him out and me and my sister and mum can live in peace."

Home worries: "Sam and his sister are my world. I can only protect them by using myself as the barrier and I cannot get out of the relationship with my partner because he said he will find us and we will regret it. No one gets it. He means it. I worry about Sam though; he is getting older and bossier and one day I'm scared he will he become like his dad."

School's viewpoint: "Sam, 14 years old, lives with his mum, dad and younger sister. As his teacher, I have never seen his dad and I always contact his mum when he has pastoral detentions or exclusions. Other kids consider him a bully and it is just a matter of time, in my opinion, before he either ends up in custody or gets thrown out of school. I wonder what is going on at home? Mum seems like a nice woman but she did look depressed when I met her earlier this year at parent's evening."

Sam's trauma: Sam exhibits violence towards more vulnerable students because he has internalized this behaviour through his repeated and consistent experience of witnessing violence from his dad. Sam may not entirely understand that the way he is displacing his anger towards his dad onto vulnerable kids is creating a path where he may end up like his dad.

Sam may not respond readily to male mentors as he has not had an experience of a good male role model and he might be very defensive. This is very unfortunate because he is in desperate need, at 14 years old, of a positive male role model.

In addition to his bullying, Sam also runs the risk of becoming a perpetrator of domestic violence as he has not only internalized the aggression of his father, but he appears to adore and to have idealized his mother and sister, and may position himself as a 'protector' of them. This is a wonderful quality but he runs the risk of not allowing his mother to have her natural and rightful parental role with him.

Sam is an adolescent and having seen over the years his mother not only brutalized and demeaned by his father, but often disempowered, may have sent the message to him that she is not an equal to his dad. In fact, today, the witnessing of domestic abuse is now recognized as a form of child abuse. The law in the UK now recognises that the domestically violent abuser can potentially have two or more victims: the one receiving the abuse and anyone witnessing it. As Sam grows up, his natural and loving instinct to protect his mother and sister may end up mixed with the misogyny he has also internalized. He might not see his mother's strength in the relationship, but unconsciously copy his dad and how he interacts with women. If this continues and is unchallenged and unsupported, Sam runs a high risk of repeating the cycle with future partners as well.

Interventions

Home: Sam's mum needs to get support for herself, Sam and his sister. For victims of domestic abuse there are support groups, such as local survivor groups that are confidential and full of (mostly) women who need a safe space to connect and share their stories. If this feels impossible for her, she should try and reach out to someone in her network, or if too isolated, then a support phone line to think through her options. There are a lot of victims out there and the best way to help her children is to give herself a lifeline first. A good analogy I always think is that of a plane, where adults are told to put their own oxygen masks on before their children's in case of an emergency. The same is true here.

As for interventions for Sam. His mum should reach out to the school, where they will have mentors and connections with mental health support/community who will help her problem solve. They are a safe place and will be ethically and legally obligated to help her. If Sam's mum found this scary, she can still reach out to an educator and ask for extra support for her son. Request a mentor for him.

School: Sam is most likely to benefit from longer-term, community-based programmes and after-school mentoring where he truly begins to internalize and challenge the entrenched violent male role model he has lived with to date. If any staff person has made a connection with Sam, use this. Reach out to that educator, regardless of their role (ignoring the hierarchy) and make a plea for Sam. One person can make an impact and begin a change within Sam. Sam needs positive male mentors, but it may not begin this way as he may only be able to relate to women as 'safe objects'. Use this to segue into a male connection.

In terms of the family, if you suspect abuse, you may be compelled to call social services. I would use a word of caution here as, in my experience, it is imperative to have a log of concrete evidence to provide social services before reporting, otherwise the situation may get worse. In the meantime, building bridges and support for Sam's mother might be invaluable because, ultimately, she has the power to change things; including leaving. Domestic violence victims all report social isolation, shame and worry about consequences, so using your own imagination about how lightly she may need to tread, may allow you to give her just enough support, in a non-judgmental manner, to get herself and her children safe. A referral to Early Help will access services, but be aware of the impact this will have on the family and try to build support for Sam and his mother, as many families feel such support adds stress to the situation.

A note on how to deal with other parents whose children may have been victim of a bully. While schools need to set limits and consequences for bullies, it can also be helpful for parents to understand that children do not become bullies from birth. They are victims themselves, and they are troubled. If you can raise other people's empathy and understanding (without betraying confidential information about the bully and their circumstances), it might help enact meaningful change for the bully. For example, if you facilitate Sam and a peer to build a positive relationship, perhaps as study partners, the link they have in class could build outside of class. This would have to be done with a lot of support and sensitivity, but bullies have been victims themselves, somewhere in their history, and this is important to remember.

> **Discussion point**
>
> Think about the bullies you know or you have known in the past. Can you think about what their 'wound' is? Did they hide it well or was it obvious? If you had thought about this aspect of their suffering, would it have changed how you approach(ed) them?

Chapter 2: Cyberbullying

Cyber-bullied: Talia

Talia's story: "I feel like killing myself. No one likes me and I feel so alone. Those girls posted that awful photo of me being kissed by those three boys at the 'sesh' (session or party) the other night and everyone is just making fun of me every day and I just can't cope. I can't go to school, I just want to cry and die. Mum is trying to talk to me, but she will just take away my phone and that won't help. Grown-ups don't understand. They think they do, but they just don't."

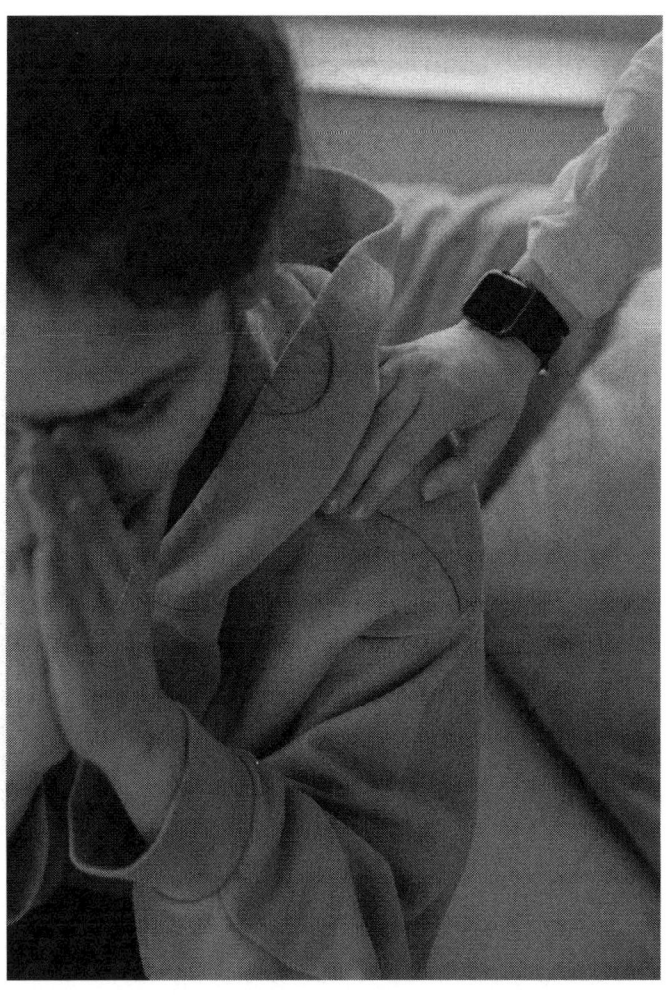

Home worries: "Talia is on her phone all the time and she just won't join us in any family activities anymore. I notice she does not have any more sleepovers and when I asked her about that, she just yelled at me and slammed her door! I told her I am going to take away her phone for a week if she continues to have this attitude with me. We are not just a hotel! She does nothing at home anymore in terms of chores and now she is also saying she does not want to go to school. When I asked her about that she refuses to talk to me. I threatened to take her phone away, as she is on it too much, and she was very over dramatic and said she would kill herself! I think that is way over the top, and told her so, but she looked so sad when she said it. Now I wonder if there if she is really feeling low. She mentioned problems at a 'sesh' but what is that anyway, and what is the big deal?"

School's viewpoint: "Talia, 15 years old, lives with mum, dad and older brother who was a great pupil here two years ago. I just heard from her science teacher that he overheard in break time that there is a photo of Talia being passed around which may be distressing to her. It seems it may be inappropriate, but I have not had a chance to check in with her yet as she seems to be absent from school today. I hope she is okay. Her family is close, so she should be fine."

Talia's Trauma: Talia was at a small party, or 'sesh', where she got very drunk and 'let' three boys kiss her. She was trying to be wild and enjoyed the attention, but is now not only regretting it but is traumatised that it has been captured and immortalized on camera, and it feels demeaning. She worries that even if she were to try and remove it, it has now been circulated. The world feels like it is caving in for Talia. She is not necessarily a 'wild' girl, but felt the pressures that so many youth feel these days keeping up with looking uninhibited on social media. She feels isolated and is filled with shame and disgust at her behaviour. She also cannot imagine that life will ever return to normal again, and that this will be the talk of the school when she returns.

Interventions

Home: Talia's parents are struggling to adapt to the pressures of parenting a modern teenager, as it departs from their own experience, and perhaps even with their older son's experience. Social media, the importance of it and the pressure of it, is alien to them and they struggle (like so many of us) to find the right balance. As with other case studies, communication is important to establish with Talia. If the lines of communication are closed, she will 'go underground'. This is not a good option for any parent. It is what all parents must avoid.

Talia's parents need to build a bridge via which they can connect her with the family on terms which feel okay to both sides, because it is likely that Talia is feeling isolated. One approach might be to have family dinner nights and TV nights. These are easy to establish and it is important that they are routine. Other ideas might be for Talia and her mum to do pamper days during which they do face scrubs and masks and watch movies together. Sports, cooking, reading the same books and discussing them are other ideas which work well. Insist on once a week.

If Talia's parents get wind of the photo, they need to contact the school in confidence and explain the situation. They need to be transparent with Talia and come up with a plan which feels acceptable to everyone. Talia will need support to return to school and maybe the family can help facilitate Talia reuniting with one or two of her more reliable friends so that she is not socially isolated. A part-time timetable to reintegrate her can also be negotiated. Social isolation and being de-schooled can be dangerous, if persistent.

Schools have an ethical and legal obligation to educate their pupils on bullying, including cyber-bullying. In addition to this, there is a really good resource: a fabulous teen-accessible play called "Girls Like That" by Evan Placey about cyber-bullying.

Never ignore suicidal gestures and threats

Suicidal threats and gestures are always cries for help. Studies show that people who feel suicidal need to be asked whether or not they want to kill themselves. Please do not use euphemisms. The following basic 'rules' around what is an extremely painful discussion include:

- **Use literal and accurate language.** Do not use figurative/euphemistic language and 'allude' to 'wanting to hurt yourself' or phrases like 'passing on'.
- **Find out if your teen has a suicide plan?** If so, what is it? Is it realistic (meaning doable and probable)?
- **If they do not have a plan, how often do they think about killing themself?** Is this just in response to this trauma, or has it happened before?
- Before ending the chat, you need to **establish a safety plan**. This plan needs to include who they will chat to if the feeling is strong when they are at home, when they are in school, and when they are out. Make sure it is reliable and doable. They also need to commit to it. Most of the time, young people only feel like they can commit to such plans (when they are feeling suicidal) for a short period of time. So have them commit to it till that evening. Then that evening, review it and commit to the next morning, etc.
- The result of this chat is for you and your teen to be very clear **on what they can do if this feeling comes again**. They may need regular and frequent check-ins. This is fine because this is a crisis and this too shall, indeed, pass.

If you can manage this conversation, you need to find your inner calm. Your aim is to 'contain' your teen and this is what they crave the most. A container for their grief, shame and embarrassment. As a parent or educator, it is amazing if you can manage this! If not, then find someone who can, with safeguarding leads at school being the first port of call. A call to CAMHS and/or a GP needs to be made and share with her/him. It is important to take all suicidal threats with plans seriously. Locate a therapist if needed. Family therapy or individual therapy can both yield a lot of help. PAPYRUS is also a resource for individuals, parents and schools for suicide prevention in teens.

> **Discussion point**
>
> Many people confuse young people wanting to 'hurt themselves' (as in self-harming) with suicide. Research shows that they are not the same thing. While a young person who wants to kill themselves may also cut themselves, if a person cuts themselves it does NOT necessarily mean they want to kill themselves. Self-harming (cutting, burning, etc) is most often a method by which to numb emotional pain (if only briefly). It does not often lead to feelings of wanting to kill themselves.
>
> This distinction is really important for adults to understand, as it can calm our emotions down when we realize these actions and thoughts are separate and distinct and not necessarily linked at all. It allows us to intervene and target the actual emotional pain of our young person.

School: Education surrounding cyber bullying is widely accessible in every school and most schools have educated their students on the subject, but it can still feel overwhelming when you are faced with it.

Part of the struggle in Talia's situation may be that some people might not see what the big deal is, after all it is just a photo of being kissed and not pornography or anything. The problem with this minimization is that we are not putting ourselves in Talia's shoes. Fitting in, convention and peer pressure are of incredible importance to many young people. Take it seriously. Also, do not assume parents know or that they can handle it, however close and loving they might appear.

Other than the school providing assistance with locating the bullies and having consequences for them, those teachers who are closest to Talia can reach out to her, gain her trust and help her to gain confidence and support whilst she rides out the storm.

Other approaches might include:

- A reminder to Talia that this will all pass. Breaking down the time and helping Talia get through each day with optional check-ins will help her immensely, as within a week or so this moment will be history.
- Connecting Talia to a few positive, strong friends. This may mean you reaching out to them which will increase her sense of support at school.
- Working with parents to help Talia back into school. Make short-term adaptions if this helps as being de-schooled for a period longer than a week can have deleterious effects.

Teachers in the classroom more generally can give all young people social and emotional activities that actually have them imagine what it might feel like to be talked about. These lessons might include that everyone will be embarrassed severely at least once in their lives, and it is important to remember what that feels like, and that we are all responsible for what we post but also what we respond to. Teachers also need to encourage leadership and take a stance against bullying, by example.

Finally, educators need to take suicidal thoughts and threats seriously, as above. Contact with parents and GPs is necessary if a young person talks about suicide. Most educators I know are very timid to act for two reasons. First, they (understandably) feel like it is too painful and worrying to handle, and fear that what they ask may trigger the young person to act. Research does not support this, though, and you need to remember that if a young person is telling you, they are consciously asking for help. You need to contact your safeguarding lead and inform them, of course, but sometimes it may lie in your lap to follow it up due to availability or urgency. Please do not worry – they are actively asking for help.

Second, educators talk about how they worry about 'betraying' the young person's confidence and 'ruining' their relationship. Whilst it is true most young people will beg you not to tell anyone, not only are you legally and ethically duty bound to tell a 'safe adult', but the act of their telling you is a cry for help. One powerful way around this feeling of betrayal is to tell them you want to be with them and will talk alongside them when you find this 'safe adult' (usually this will be the safeguarding lead who will then take charge).

The young person will often tell you they are angry with you and will never talk to you again, but you need to trust that you are (a) doing the right thing and (b) your relationship will recuperate in time; remember that they approached you to begin with and this is a huge act of trust. To fail in this duty not only potentially runs the risk of a terrible outcome for the young person, but also by failing to act you are actually not responding in the way the young person expected you to. Young people, for all their pleas to the contrary, know very well that when they talk to an adult they trust and who is reliable, that adult will act accordingly. By not acting, you are potentially breaking their trust and this is a huge breach of boundaries.

> **Discussion point**
>
> It is interesting to note that most bullies were bullied themselves. Sometimes the bully has been bullied at home, other times they have been victims of bullying at school. The transition often happens when the young person enters a scary environment, such as a larger secondary school, where the protections that might have been present (such as a protective teacher) are lost in the vastness of the new school. Social groups also shift when entering a new and larger school, so the already fragile system of support of the bullied can fail. Some decide to become the aggressor to protect themselves, rather than succumb to more bullying. If you want, ask your teen what they think of this. I bet they know of some examples.

Chapter 3: Parental abuse and neglect

Ellie's story: "I can't concentrate on maths, I just need to know when I can get out of here. My arm aches where Mum yanked me out of bed this morning; I didn't want to come. What's the point of school, anyway? How can I learn when all I can do is hear my tummy growl? There are some lunch boxes in that corner over there. When no one is watching, I am going to grab the crisps and biscuits. The others make fun of me. I know I stink. Mum tells me I am a 'loser' and 'stupid'. She's right. I am not going to say anything. I hate social workers. I will just get sent away. I'm just a loser anyway. No one cares."

Home worries: "Ellie thinks she has it rough, well she did not have my upbringing! She reminds me of myself and I am trying to set her right but she just never listens to me. She needs to toughen up, if not she will end up like me with kids, no money, no job and no man. No one gets my pain and I am trying my best for Ellie and my kids."

School's viewpoint: "Ellie, 13 years old, has very few friends and looks dirty and unkempt. She is very thin and exhibits a poor attention span. She is very quiet in class and seems like she has a learning disability, but the school has never gotten to the bottom of it. She lives at home with her single mum and is the eldest of six siblings.

She talks to no one. I am worried about her and have approached her, but she is evasive. I have nicknamed her the 'invisible kid' as she seems to pop up in places and also disappears when you think she is there. I really feel for her, but I don't know where to begin."

Ellie's trauma: Ellie is physically and emotionally neglected and abused. She lives in poverty and her mother is likely to have been a victim of abuse and neglect in her own childhood. Her mum's poor parenting skills are aggravated by their poverty, lack of meaningful support, and Ellie's new adolescent sense of autonomy. Ellie's self-esteem is extremely low as she has internalized all the hurtful messages given to her at home, which are amplified by her peers who mock her.

Ellie not only struggles with the actual trauma of abuse and neglect but is socially isolated. She is a teenager where outside appearance and material wealth are more focused on than when she was younger. Her unkempt appearance will alienate her from most of her peers. She may be prone to telling 'tall tales' with peers as she overcompensates and pretends to her peers that her life is fuller than it is. When Ellie describes her 'cool' bedroom she has equipped with the latest technology and decor, her peers brand her as a 'liar' because they know that these descriptions do not match up to her general appearance.

Interventions

Home: As a parent, Ellie's mum need support. Building bridges with school will be a good starting point. Most parents who have suffered abuse in their childhood have little faith in school and social work systems. They have a history of being failed and it is quite obvious from how Ellie's mum treats her that she has not received the help she has needed in the past. Poverty is also a huge difficulty Ellie's mum has to face, which impacts not only on her day-to-day living but also on her mental health. She might respond to someone in the school staff who she relates to. Often this is not a teacher, but a teaching assistant or mentor. Perhaps someone who has shared a similar past, so she does not feel judged and more inadequate than she already feels.

School: As mentioned above, Ellie's mum might respond to someone on your school staff when building some support for her. All too often, parents like to focus on their children as the 'problems' as it is too painful to own much of this responsibility themselves. It feels overwhelming and it probably is. So baby steps are needed. Approach Ellie's mum carefully and slowly build up trust before offering her support which might even have practical applications, like linking her up to free food resources in the community or offering her parent drop-in sessions where she can have a chat and coffee. If you can get through to her mum, you can potentially help Ellie (and all of Ellie's siblings who, without intervention, will likely follow in Ellie's footsteps).

Social workers should be used if you have solid and repeated evidence of neglect and abuse. The reality, however, is that social workers are totally overstretched and it is unlikely they will be well received by Ellie's mum and her involvement may be perceived by her as punitive in nature. Try to offer a gentle and supportive relationship towards her mum, to help her improve Ellie's care as this will help Ellie more than a social worker. Of course, if abuse if happening then you must report it, but know that the chance of Ellie moving to a safer home is unlikely to work because (a) very few foster homes exist for teenagers and the home situation needs to be totally untenable before a social worker will explore this option; and (b) many teenagers will opt to stay in their (abusive/neglectful) home environments over the fear of a new home. Also, for all the abuse Ellie has experienced, she is still likely to be very loyal to her mother (either by fear and/or by very low self-confidence after years of being told she is a 'loser', which she has internalized).

One option the school can provide outside the home environment is a separate space where Ellie can experience being 'seen' for who she is. Ellie may be a gifted artist, good in English or sciences, or a really compassionate person. She will likely be resistant at first, but slowly building a trusting relationship (a bit like with mum) based on some of her obvious strengths will be worth a try. Expect resistance as Ellie will expect to be rejected, and so she will reject you first in order to protect herself.

Traumatised young people often have very low self-esteem and will reject the adults trying to help them. Often this resistance is vociferous and entrenched. They say they want to be rid of you. The truth is, however, they are afraid to hope that your interest in them is for real. They are masking their hope that they will receive unconditional acceptance, but they are far too fragile emotionally to ask for this. If we are honest and look within ourselves, the act of asking for unconditional love or acceptance makes us very vulnerable. Most of us would struggle with this. A child with Ellie's history will really struggle with it, so please persist!

Another possible intervention is pairing Ellie up with a peer who is kind and compassionate. This peer might help Ellie build bridges with other peers. Offering group or individual support to mum could help. Finally, any social work involvement needs to be done very carefully and only if there is very solid, documented and long-term evidence of neglect/abuse; if not, Ellie might suffer more at home.

Discussion point

The cloak of 'invisibility' is not uncommon with traumatised young people. Can you think of an adolescent who might not be as difficult or demanding, but is perhaps falling through the cracks? As a parent, you might have one child that is less demanding emotionally: do you balance the attention across all your children, or focus on the most demanding? As an educator, there are most definitely young people in your classes who are 'invisible' and not discussed. Can you work out who they are? If so, perhaps focus your next staff meeting on their needs, rather than the ones whose behaviours demand it.

Chapter 4: Identity issues

Lack of ethnic/cultural identity role models: Tyree

Tyree's story: "I never met my dad, and I don't have any contact with that side of my family. People say my dad used to beat my mum up. That's why I never met him. I hate him, I think he's a piece of shit. My mum's white and dad's black. Everyone around me is white, except my best mate, Shaun. I am not sure what I want to do with my life. I'm no good at football or rapping. The other day my mates said Hasna only liked me because she's into 'black guys'. I don't know what to think. I thought we got on so well. Does she really only like me because I am black? Is that all that I am to her?"

Home worries: "My boy, Tyree, is my heart. He is such a good boy but I worry that he has never met his dad. I am aware that most stories about his dad depict him as a bad person, but recently his dad wanted to meet up with him and I just do not know what to do. Tyree says there is no way he will meet his dad, so what am I to do? I know Tyree has had it rough at times. I realise it is not easy to have just me and my family around him, but what should I do? He needs a male role model, but his dad will probably not follow through and I worry what will happen. His dad was not easy and he hit me. I know I don't need him in my life, but does Tyree?"

School's viewpoint: Tyree, 15 years old, looks indifferent a lot of the time. Occasionally, he can look upset. He lives at home with his mum, younger brother and older sister. Tyree has a few friends who seem really tight with him, though he is often truant and does not attend class enough. Girls seem to love him and his attitude. I have tried to talk to him but he just shuts me out. Once I saw him crying and I approached him and he told me to 'F---- off' and asked how I could understand anyway since I am 'just a white guy'."

Tyree's Trauma: Tyree is not only suffering from a lack of immediate positive role models, which he is seeking as a 'normal' adolescent, but he struggles with society's definitions about what it is to be a black male. When his friends said Hasna 'only likes black guys', it reduces his whole self to a skin colour in a way that other people are not similarly stereotyped. It is not only reductive, but it chips away at his self-esteem and reinforces his already poor sense of self and identity.

Tyree carries a trauma that has been societally reinforced in the day to day. So is it surprising that he has an exaggerated response when daily events trigger him? Perhaps a white boy who had not grown up with all these negative images of his ethnic and cultural identity would have had a lesser response?

Interventions

Home: Tyree's mum might look into other ways she might help Tyree explore his identity, in addition to connecting him to real life mentors. Cultural identity can be explored through the media, looking at black men who have made a difference and are good role models in whatever field of interest Tyree has. Music, film and sport models are readily available, but also every domain, whether it is finance, business, law, politics, social work or whatever, will have strong black men who lead in some capacity. Follow them in the social media, talk about their TED talks and use this to indirectly influence Tyree and his image, which may be narrow due to his perception of his father.

As for whether or not to 'allow' contact with his father, Tyree needs to be part of an honest, open discussion about the risks. Plans need to be made to manage potential disappointments and Tyree needs to assert his preferences to his dad, if indeed he is to see him again. Other male role models can also be asked to step up. Yes, ideally there will be some role models who are similar to him ethnically, but more importantly Tyree's journey is to manhood and all role models are helpful. The role-model relationship needs to be independent from the home with activities like bike rides, movies, shared moments, but without the parent.

School: Interventions at school need to focus on identity. Identity in all its forms: cultural, ethnic, spiritual, gender, etc. Curiosity in discussions and lessons on different influences can be reinforced as often these sorts of discussions can show there are links between both students and teachers which may not already have been apparent.

The theory of intersectionality

While we are thinking about ethnic and cultural identity, there is an interesting theory which might help bridge cultures, backgrounds and ethnicities together: intersectionality.

Thirty years ago, Kimberlé Crenshaw coined the concept of intersectionality: how race, gender, class, sexuality and immigrant status 'intersect and often overlap one another'. People will identify with aspects of their cultural, ethnic, gender and other identities, which will, or will not, be visible to others. This theory can be useful for helping Tyree and his classmates as it unites people in their 'differences' rather than divides them. This might help Tyree's classes develop a more supportive, inclusive and psychologically minded school culture that embraces difference as a source of strength, diversity and empowerment. With this spirit, educators can discuss the positive and negative aspects of their own identity, adopting a spirit of transparency and openness (but being mindful of boundaries).

Other interventions which could help Tyree might include:

- Identify and acknowledge his strengths. His popularity and attitude demonstrate good social skills and probably charisma, which can be supported and developed into leadership qualities.
- Help him understand where his hurt and anger come from. Affirm his right to his feelings and explain that he has choices in how he expresses them.
- Help him with grounding techniques to support him when triggered. There will be a chapter later on in this book listing grounding techniques that can be explored at school or at home.

Finally, any way in which the school can support Tyree with both individual and group supports in the community and out of school will help him immensely. Any programme that promotes positive role models can only benefit Tyree.

Discussion point

In order for us to progress at home, at school, in our communities on the issues of identity, ethnicity, gender, sexuality etc, we can initiate non-judgmental conversations with our children, students and friends. What is usually interesting is how diverse people feel internally, when pushed to explore all the childhood influences they may have had. This is not to reduce everyone's experience to being the same, but when we can genuinely embrace our differences, it can be the beginning of us uniting over change and difference, rather than feeling separate because of difference.

Gender identity and sexuality issues: Jac

Jac's story: "Mum and dad still call me Emily but my name is now Jac to my friends. I have always felt like I was different and I just know I am a boy, but my parents are not ready to hear this. My mum looks at me every time a gay kid walks by, but she just never talks to me about it. I am not sure she even knows the difference between being gay and trans. I am not even sure my dad sees it. Most of my friends are cool with it. Not that I have many, but that's ok. School does these lectures and have now branded some bathrooms as gender neutral, but I still feel like most of them don't get how much it is in my head all the time. How can I focus on schoolwork when I

Chapter 4: Identity issues

am dealing with much bigger things? I have changed my name for my friends, but teachers and family don't know it. To them I am Emily, but to me, I am Jac."

Home worries: Emily is such a bright girl! She has always been top of her class and she has always been a bit of an introvert, really. Emily doesn't have many friends, but she seems to have a few good ones and that is what counts, I suppose. She blew up at dad the other day when he asked her if James was her boyfriend and I do think she is wondering if she is gay or not. When she was little she never wanted girly clothes, but what does that matter, anyway? She has seemed more secretive as of late, come to think of it. But she is 16 and I think that is normal. I don't see her date anyone, not that I would have a problem with her being gay, I just think too much pressure is put on kids to decide about their sexuality. The other day it seemed like she wanted to tell me something when I suggested she wear a dress just for her cousin's wedding, but she just slammed her door and that was that. Anyway, I guess she will come to me if she wants to."

School's viewpoint: "Emily/Jac, 16 years old, is the eldest of three children who live with both parents in a middle-class neighbourhood. They look like an average intact family, without any worrying signs from the school's perspective. Emily is down on paper as 'Emily' but I hear her friends call her 'Jac' and using they/their pronouns. Her parents seem to use the name Emily, at least at the last parent's evening, so I am not sure what is up with that? Emily has seemed less happy lately and dresses more boyishly; I wonder if she is exploring their sexuality? I suppose as long as Emily keeps up with her work then there will be no problem. I did notice her sobbing in the courtyard the other day, and when I approached her, she hurried away. I wonder if I should talk to Emily's parents about this, and about the other name?"

Jac's trauma: Jac appears to be exploring both their gender identity and their sexuality. Due to society's strong views on 'trans' acceptance (which are only beginning to evolve meaningfully in some parts of the UK) and their parent's lack of curiosity, Jac's internal identity crisis around their gender and sexuality is hidden to most. Jac is likely experiencing some 'gender dysmorphia', which is a feeling of distress or discomfort around a shifting gender identity from the one assigned at birth. Jac may become a transgender or gender non-conforming person, or they may not. Jac is only 16 years old and is clearly exploring all aspects of their gender and sexuality and could really benefit from meaningful support both at home and at school.

Jac may not understand their feelings and has felt drawn to identifying as a boy for a very long time, but has not been able to express it as they might have expressed other needs. The messages their family, friends and community have been implicitly sending since Jac was a baby conform to heterosexual norms. Regardless of our own personal thoughts about gender exploration, most of us should be able to accept that it would be incredibly difficult and confusing for anyone who feels this way. If we are to take our own sense of current morality and values away, we can challenge ourselves to just sit with the thought that it must be really, really hard for Jac. Not only does Jac have all the normal 16-year-old pressures to grow up, get educated and fulfil themselves – but they are also feeling like a 'he' or a 'they'.

> **Discussion point**
>
> Can you challenge yourself to really think about what it might feel like for Jac? Just imagine being the opposite gender than you are. What would it feel like? What would be the good bits and bad bits?
>
> Now imagine you want to be this other gender. How would that feel in your body? How would you relate to others? How difficult might it be to convey this to others? Who would you find it easiest to tell and hardest to tell? Why do you think that is? Would you feel supported or ashamed? How would it feel to be called 'they' and have people stumble over the word every time they use it?
>
> Now just imagine having to wake up and on top of all the normal issues you might have to face in your day, to actually have this basic worry to contend with. All day long. All night long. No respite. That might help us understand what it is like for someone like Jac, who is only 16 years old.

Interventions

Home: Emily/Jac needs her/their parents to pick up the social clues they will have given at home and become more curious about their inner life. Too often families discount a lot of worrying behaviours under the umbrella of 'adolescent' behaviours. How many times have you heard (or said), 'Oh she/he was just being a normal teenager!' This usually elicits chuckles or nods of understanding.

Though this may be true, many families discount a lot of warning signs and worries their young people have. An occasional sign of anger and distress is totally normal for all of us, and yes, probably pronounced in teenagers who are trying to individuate from us and also have high levels of hormones flying through their bodies. But if a pattern or theme comes up, please do not ignore it!

In this case, it is likely that Jac's parents have heard people call their daughter 'Jac' – heard it or seen it on a text or an email. Also, they are likely to have given hundreds of hints and signals beyond the obvious insistence on clothing and such. If your adolescent slams the door when you ask what appears to be an inoffensive question, approach them and talk about it. Too many adolescents go 'underground' and hide things from parents and they actually think the parents won't understand. Too often we, as parents, forget what it felt like to be an adolescent and how conflicted and aimless most of us felt at that time. Use your memory and remember how it actually felt to be 16 years old. Most of us had struggles.

Jac is struggling with big issues here. These are not tiffs with friends, which also should not be ignored if they are too regular or there is a pattern of rejection. It is likely that Jac's parents have picked up their gender identity and sexuality issues, but maybe fear or the hope that it is just a 'passing phase' has inhibited them from having the difficult conversations.

This is understandable, but they need to support Jac who is in significant distress. As their parent, it is not only their responsibility but they genuinely know their child and can offer them support which is different to anything Jac can get elsewhere: it is precious and long-term. If not, Jac will start going through this and many other things under the radar and their parents will lose an important chance to help with Jac's exploration, wherever it leads.

School: Schools often are quite good at addressing gender identity and sexual issues in bigger assemblies, but translating this learning to meaningful thought which can actually help young people who are struggling is more of a challenge. In this journey, providing Jac with school and community support is key. A combination of a school mentor and helping them link up with relevant groups within the community can be helpful.

Talking in private to Jac and helping them link with their family would also be an excellent intervention. Sometimes, young people can really benefit having an educator as a facilitator for a tricky discussion with a family member. Having transparency across a number of support systems for Jac would be the most important thing, including discussions on how to best support them at school if their grades appear to be sliding a bit. Acknowledging how difficult and burdensome their challenge is can also alleviate a lot of stress for Jac. With support and acknowledgement from the school, community and home, Jac will feel more connected and this will likely lead to improvement in their wellbeing.

Finally, there are many resources on the internet that are very supportive for LGBTQ+ youth. One such resource is Courageous Leaders, which supports and promotes teachers to be open about their gender and sexual identities in an appropriate manner, which helps support open discussions with the aim of increasing young people's confidence around their identity. The website is: http://www.courageousleaders.org.uk.

Chapter 5: Body image disorder

Body Dysmorphic Disorder (BDD): Jazz

Jazz's story: "I look like a freak. I cannot bear it. Mum and my friends make fun of me because they say I look in the mirror all the time, but they just don't get it. I hate my skin. I mean I really HATE its colour, texture, and the fact I am so pasty. No treatment I do helps me. I have tried about 100 skin creams, but nothing helps. If anyone posts a pic of me on social media I literally die inside. And no way am I looking at myself on online classes. Not with my camera on. If I do that, then I just cannot concentrate on anything and it makes me feel sick to my stomach. My parents and teachers just don't get it. They think I am using it as an excuse not to engage with online classes. They don't get it. I am so ugly. There is nothing I can do about it. Everyone around me just minimizes it and says I am vain, but I'm not. I can't manage my homework because all I think about it how I am going to face school the next day."

Home worries: "Jazz is such a lovely girl, I don't understand why she seems to focus so much on her skin? Not to show off, but she really is a beautiful girl. When she first started I supported her with her skin regime, as that's just good adolescent cleansing regime, but lately it's out of control! I actually caught her buying a skin scar repair cream which she spread across her face, but she doesn't have any scars?! She also refuses to post any photos of herself, which is great on the one hand, but her friends seem to find this odd. I am at a loss as to what to do with her. Dad just thinks she is vain and scolds her when she doesn't participate in online classes more actively, but

I'm beginning to wonder if this is really about her looks or something deeper. She also seems to have problems doing her homework and seems consumed with watching those video bloggers on make-up instead."

School's viewpoint: "Jazz, 13 years old, lives with her parents and her older brother and sister. Jazz is a somewhat confusing girl. She had excellent predicted grades from primary school, but just seems to be very low in participation and effort in class. It's not like she has an attitude, rather she appears quite sweet and quiet, but I can't seem to motivate her to increase her work output. When I asked her about the lack of quality in her homework she seemed tearful and barely responded. She appears unhappy but I can't figure out why as she's struggling so much. I've noticed she has recently put on a lot of make-up, including lots of foundation even though she doesn't appear to have acne, but she's not alone in this as so many 13 year old's seem to experiment with make-up. I'm not sure what is going on."

Jazz's Trauma: BDD stands for Body Dysmorphic Disorder. It is the huge preoccupation with a perceived flaw in one's appearance. BDD usually focuses on one or two body parts, like skin, hair, nose, eyes, scars, eyebrows, chin, breasts, genitals, stomach, height, etc. It can be on any facet of someone's appearance and it is often confused with vanity or over-concern with superficiality; but it is not.

BDD usually starts in adolescence and its root causes are not yet known. Biological, trauma/psychological and societal (media and cultural messages) are being explored as causes for this disorder. It often leads to anxiety, depression and feelings of shame, and can severely impact normal functioning in our lives. It affects men and women alike. If your teen spends over an hour on her/his appearance, then they may be at risk of BDD. About 2% of the population has this disorder. So, Jazz's trigger for this trauma may be unknown.

BDD includes issues around:

- **Unanswerable questions:** She has a distorted view of her physique and continuously focuses on her appearance, so she wonders why she has these problems when others don't.
- **Self-criticism:** I think most of us can identify a critical voice inside of us. At times this voice is based on reality (we know when we have messed up, for example), and at other times it is more based on our fears or our insecurities (like when we berate ourselves for being too forward with someone or too withholding and we just 'know' we have blown the encounter). Here, Jazz has the second type of persecutory inner voice which criticizes her appearance all the time. It ends up distorted and not based on reality. Beliefs like, 'My skin is too pale or too bumpy', or 'I am defective' are inner dialogues she has all the time.
- **Fantasies:** People with BDD can fantasize, for example those who get addicted to plastic surgery can be victims of this, focusing on one 'defect' after another. Jazz believes if she changes something about her skin she will no longer be unhappy and that she will fit in with her peers and find inner happiness.

- **Negative comparisons:** Jazz is very good at seeing other people's positive traits and then comparing her own to them in a negative way. For example, she sees her friend's clear skin and then sees only faults in her own.
- **Overgeneralisations:** Jazz fills her mind with assertions like 'never', 'always', 'entire', 'all', and 'every', which are overgeneralizations. For example, 'I am always the dumbest in the class' or, Jazz's case, 'My skin is never okay'.
- **Worries:** Jazz fills her mind with 'what if' scenarios that plague her mind and fill it with worries which reinforce her feelings of powerlessness. For example, "What if I am like this forever?' or 'I can never change'.
- **Negative reflections and distortions:** Jazz looks back at events or things she has done and feels like her poor decisions have a long-standing or unchanging impact on her life. For example, in Jazz thinks, 'If I hadn't used all those creams, then my skin would be nice; now it's ruined forever'. Also, Jazz denigrates or reduces other people's positive comments about her and distorts the intent of them. For example, she thinks, 'My friends said I looked nice at the party, not because I did but because they felt sorry for me'.
- **Distressing images:** Jazz also has false images of how she is perceived by other people. People with BDD report they often have actual images in their minds of how someone else's eye perceives them. This is obviously interpreted by how they perceive themselves and not others, but can be very painful.

Interventions

Home: Treatment for this disorder includes pharmacology (medication) and Cognitive Behavioural Therapy (CBT). As parents, if Jazz's parents pick up the symptoms above and it is inhibiting her normal functioning, such as attending school and socializing, it is time to seek outside treatment with a CBT therapist and/or a psychiatrist who can prescribe SSRIs – medication that helps with serotonin levels. They can also help support Jazz at home. The following link has an excellent free workbook which focuses on the symptoms and strategies which you can download and print out:

BDD Resource: www.cci.health.wa.gov.au/-/media/CCI/Consumer-Modules/Building-Body-Acceptance/Building-Body-Acceptance---03---Reducing-Appearance-Preoccupation.pdf

The key for parents is not to minimize the symptoms and understand that the healing process will take a while.

School: Jazz, like many teens with BDD, struggles with school. She is consumed by her preoccupation and this interrupts her daily life and may make her late to class, be disorganized with homework and worry about any participation in class. Reaching out to her and her parents would be a good first step.

Jazz needs more support in her classes, and perhaps creating more support and mentoring around academic success might uncover some of the underlying issues she is struggling with. Most of the interventions for BDD are CBT based, so if a relationship is developed between an educator and Jazz, then as much reinforcement of positive thinking as possible and encouraging her to gently question her misconceptions would help her enormously. At 13 years old, Jazz will be looking for role models outside of her family circle and the school is well placed to provide these.

> **Discussion point**
>
> I chose BDD over other body image disorders like anorexia and bulimia as I thought it was less known and yet quite similar in its manifestation. People often confuse these body image disorders with 'superficiality' as they are often linked to societal values of beauty. Most of us have parts of ourselves which we do not like and wish could be different. What do you think makes the difference between this dislike and a more profound hatred for parts of ourselves? Can you imagine how hard it would be if you thought about this body part all day and night? It would be unlikely that you could moderate your dislike for this body part with a sense of humour or a shrug. What role do you think social media has in this disorder?

Chapter 6: The trauma of (undiagnosed) mental health issues

Undiagnosed Autism Spectrum Condition (ASC): Zac

Zac's story: "I keep getting into trouble at school and I don't know why. I banter with kids and they just don't get it. I know I push it too far sometimes, but don't they see I am just having a little fun? No one sticks to me, except my two mums. My little brother has a lot of friends so I don't know why I can't manage to keep them? Mum has them over to hang out and we play footie outside, but then mum says I am just much too much for them, and they end up dumping me and I have to move on. Mum says I can be obsessional, but I don't really know what she means. School is a drag, and when it gets too noisy I just have to check out. It stresses me out."

Home worries: "I am worried about Zac. I worry so much about how he is doing in school, even though he is academic, he doesn't get along with many kids at all. He often only focuses on one friend and then overwhelms him and then gets dumped. He has never been invited to birthday parties or homes much like the other kids. It breaks my heart. I do try and tell Zac to diversify his friends but he does not seem to be able to. This has always been the case since he was little. And he is so literal! I think he misses the point a lot when he tries to 'banter' with his friends. I am so worried that one day he will get kicked out of school as he has begun to get to more physical in his 'bantering.'"

School's viewpoint: "Zac, 13 years old, lives with two mums and has a younger brother. His home appears intact and loving. Zac is a very clever boy but he is not easy to have in my class. He does not listen to me often and appears to be very literal in his understanding of things. He doesn't have many friends and some kids shun him, it seems. The other day, when I was trying to break up a situation between Zac and his two friends, which looked to me like it might tip to violence, Zac was the only one who just did not seem to 'get it', if you see what I mean? In that instance he pushed his friend away and thought it was funny, but his friend clearly did not. I did explain to Zac that physical aggression cannot be tolerated in our school, but he just walked away! There a history of Zac getting into low grade arguments with his peers so I'm not surprised, though the physicality is a new thing, I think?"

Zac's trauma: Zac suffers from the trauma of being undiagnosed and he is a likely candidate for being assessed for Autism Spectrum Condition (ASC) because of his significant and ongoing social communication problems, which have plagued him since he was a little child. It has likely been missed as he has been raised in a loving home and is above average intelligence which has masked his social interaction and communication problems.

ASC is a condition some people are born with and it affects how they interact with others and process information. Zac's school has missed his symptoms as he has always done well academically and because his mothers have been very proactive, they have helped mitigate his social interactions. As Zac is getting to be an adolescent, however, more independent and seeking less family input (in an age-appropriate manner), he is likely to get into more 'trouble' and this can lead to problems. His trauma has to do with carrying the narrative that he is a 'bad kid' with his peers and he is socially isolated. Had his ASC been diagnosed earlier, then measures in school and at home could have been put in place to help Zac thrive rather than struggle with his ASC.

The Australian Parenting website, Raising Children, provides a really clear and comprehensive list of ASC symptoms which can be found in teens. This is useful as a lot of ASC material is geared to younger children. Their website is: https://raisingchildren.net.au/autism. They break down areas of difficulty in a helpful manner: verbal and non-verbal communication, relationships, repetitive behaviours and sensory sensitivities. This list of ASC symptoms includes:

Verbal communication issues:

- Having trouble taking turns in conversations – for example, they might like to do all the talking or find it hard to answer questions about themselves.
- Talking a lot about favourite topics, but finding it difficult to talk about a range of topics.
- Being confused by language and take things literally – for example, they might be confused by the expression 'Pull your socks up!' and actually pull up their socks.
- Having an unusual tone of voice, or use speech in an unusual way – for example, they might speak very loudly, or in a monotonous voice or with an accent.
- Having a very good vocabulary and talking in formal, old-fashioned ways.
- Finding it hard to follow instructions with more than one or two steps.

Nonverbal communication:

▶ Having trouble reading nonverbal cues, like body language or tone of voice, to guess how someone else is feeling – for example, they might not understand when adults are angry based on their tone of voice, or they might not be able to tell when someone is teasing them or using sarcasm.
▶ Using eye contact in an unusual way – for example, they might make less eye contact than others, or not use eye contact when they're spoken to.
▶ Expressing few emotions on their faces, or being unable to read other people's facial expressions – for example, they might not be able to tell whether someone likes them in a romantic way.
▶ Using very few gestures to express themselves.

Developing relationships:

▶ Preferring to spend time on their own rather than with their peers.
▶ Needing other children to play by their rules and get upset if their rules aren't followed.
▶ Having trouble understanding the social rules of friendship.
▶ Having difficulty making friends and have few or no real friends.
▶ Having trouble relating to children their own age and prefering to play with younger children or adults.
▶ Having difficulty adjusting their behaviour in different social situations.
▶ Invading others' personal space by getting too close to them.

Repetitive behaviour and interests:

▶ Having unusual interests or obsessions – for example, they might collect sticks or memorise football statistics but not really be interested in the game.
▶ Having compulsive behaviours – for example, they might line things up or need to close all the doors in the house.
▶ Having an unusual attachment to objects – for example, they might carry toys around, or collect unusual items like chip packets or shoelaces.
▶ Being easily upset by change and like to follow routines – for example, they might like to sit in the same seat for every meal or have a special order for getting ready in the morning.
▶ Repeating body movements or have unusual body movements, like hand-flapping or rocking.
▶ Making repetitive noises – for example, grunts, throat-clearing or squealing.

Sensory sensitivities:

▶ Being sensitive to sensory experiences – for example, they might be easily upset by certain sounds like the ticking of a clock or uncomfortable clothes like shoes that are too tight or never quite right, or they may only eat only foods with a certain texture.
▶ Seeking sensory stimulation – for example, they might like deep pressure, seek vibrating objects like washing machines, or flutter fingers to the sides of their eyes to watch the light flicker.

- ▶ Being less responsive or more responsive to pain than other children.
- ▶ Noise/smells/touch can be very overwhelming and you notice their mood changes as a result of them.

These are some of the symptoms but it is not an exhaustive list. If your young person has a lot of these, it may be worth investigating. I have been struck at how ASC can be missed, especially when families have been loving and good at caring which can lead to school and parents not realizing there is an underlying problem, and once the person is an adolescent, out of the family cocoon, problems flourish.

Interventions

Home: Zac's parents should take him to a psychiatrist or CAMHS (Child and Adolescent Mental Heath Services) for an assessment and/or diagnosis. Many parents/carers understandably wonder whether or not it is worth getting their child diagnosed. Of course, everyone may have different thoughts on this but it can be helpful because:

- ▶ Having a diagnosis will allow you to access more support.
- ▶ Though there is stigma associated to most mental health labels, let us be honest, the young person will likely feel quite a bit of relief when they know that they are not just 'bad' but that there is a reason for their behaviours. This is not to be confused with the diagnosis allowing them to stop taking responsibility for any their behaviours. Rather, it can help others understand the challenges they face and how to improve communication with them.

How the diagnosis is communicated to Zac is critical. It needs to be understood that it is not dooming him in any way and that there a large numbers of highly successful (in all senses of the word) people out there. Indeed, this diagnosis, like many others, has some positive points, such as creativity and a 'specialist' brain which can lead to being expert in a future profession/job. It can help to give families and schools tools to help Zac so that he works towards independent living and building better self-esteem.

> My Ace Space (MAS) is a new resource for young teenagers but could be adapted to older ones and is worth looking at as it is really innovative and helpful if your teen struggles with sensory issues. The strategies offered are easily adapted to older teens
>
> It is a system that helps children aged 7-13 to develop their emotional and sensory regulation, developing skills to manage anger, frustration and boredom. MAS consists of training for parents, teachers and carers, digital content/app for children and adults to use as well as a community to create an environment where neurodiverse children can thrive. The training is delivered online through manageable, bite-sized lessons. The app will allow children to identify what state they are in, be nudged towards possible solutions to help manage their situation and encourage them to get to a state where they are calmer, more alert and engaged. MAS combines experts from education and occupational therapy to further develop a tried and tested system that has already benefited 1000s of young people.
>
> Website: www.myacespace.co.uk

School: The three educational areas Zac will struggle with at school include social interaction, communication and imagination. As the ASC has been undiagnosed until adolescence, it is unlikely that any/many strategies in place to compensate for the difficulties in these domains. Sensory difficulties (noise, touch, smells and textures, in particular) are likely to overwhelm Zac, though he is likely to be unaware of this. Kids with ASC report that such sensory problems inhibit their ability to access lessons due to poorer concentration as they are distracted by their sensory overload. Zac may also present as emotionally rigid – this is not 'being difficult' but rather his way of managing sensory and social overload. Any of us, when genuinely overwhelmed, naturally focus on what we think is most 'important' to help us manage; people with ASC have to cope with this all of the time.

So, what are some strategies that might help Zac in school?

First it is imperative that you meet with his parents and get a better understanding of what 'works' for Zac. Too often we look at what does not work, but actually looking at what helps can guide us to better strategies. See what helps at home as this can help guide classroom accommodations. Here are some suggestions:

▶ See if there is a seat that makes him more comfortable. It may be away from noise, or somewhere he feels more separate from others or closer to the teacher.
▶ People with ASC often respond very well to visual timetables and cues, as words can be confusing at times. They also show a visual structure which feels containing and safer.
▶ Come up with strategies for when he is feeling distressed. It can be a word or a visual cue (like a red pen) which he uses when distressed. Then have a specific agreement about where her can go or what he does to help him.
▶ Identify one key person/mentor at school who Zac can check in with once a day as this consistency will help him.
▶ Use literal language as much as possible and explain when you have to use figurative language.
▶ Zac may struggle with changes in routine, such as school trips and such. Discussions about this and plans need to be put in place beforehand with Zac and his parents.
▶ Introduce an 'activity-brief' plan where you: (a) provide a visual itinerary for the day and go through it step-by-step beforehand (preferably, well in advance); (b) during the day, check-in and remind him subtly where they are (being mindful of finding a moment when peers are not around so he will not feel shamed) and (c) if Zac feels it is helpful, go through a summary of the day and identify with him what worked well and where he may have struggled; and (d) rework the plan with Zac for the next itinerary so as to integrate his feedback but make it as predictable and consistent as possible.
▶ Do not expect Zac to make eye contact and let him know this.
▶ Help Zac have a study buddy – perhaps someone who struggles in areas that Zac does not and who is strong where Zac is not. So this person might benefit from some study support but might be stronger, socially. It would need to be a compassionate person, and perhaps a girl, so that Zac does not compare himself to this person in a linear way.

- ▶ Break class activities into small groups because this will be far less overwhelming for Zac (and may benefit other kids as well).
- ▶ Overall, Zac will respond to more structure and routine in any ways you can provide this.

> **Discussion point**
>
> Pick something you are really bad at. For example, if you are right-handed, having to write and draw all day long with your left hand, with no exceptions. Or if you wear glasses, do not wear the glasses all day long. Then imagine being in school and being asked to use the skill you do not have at all, and that this is your new status quo.
>
> How does this feel? Do you feel inadequate, disempowered or just really incapable of doing even the most basic tasks?
>
> Well, this gives us a taste of what it might feel like for a young person who has ASC and is asked to interact in highly social and socialized circles all day long at school. Or someone with dyslexia who is asked to write all day long.
>
> How exhausted would you feel at the end of the day? How 'stupid' or incapable would you feel in contrast to everyone else?

Chapter 7: Social isolation

Isolation: Saul

Saul's story: "I know that everyone is going through what I'm going through, but I just feel like I can't cope. I feel like I can't complain to my friends because they are going through it too, and what's the big deal? I'm having trouble sleeping and I don't go to bed before 5am most nights, so when I have 8:30am classes online, I just sleep through them. My dad's on my case because he thinks I am just being lazy but all I think about is whether anyone I care about going to die I used to be a party boy and the life of any party! I was on the school rugby team but now I do no sport except once in a while throw a ball around with a single friend in the park. Now when I see my friends, which is very rare, I just feel disconnected with them. I just don't know if I will ever graduate. What's the point anyway as there are no jobs out there and this virus is just the first of many, so why bother?"

Home worries: "Saul used to be the easiest kid ever! He was easy going, fun, well-liked and decent at school. Now it is all going downhill. I mean, I know it is difficult for him, like everyone else, but he just needs to get on with it. Why can he not join classes like all of the other kids do? I know not seeing friends must be difficult for him, but like I said, it's hard for everyone. We just need to pull up our socks and get on with it. I offered to bring him to the park near some of his friends who live farther away but he just shrugs and says, 'What's the point?' In fact that is his answer for everything these days."

School's viewpoint: "Saul, 15 years old, lives with dad, mum and two siblings. Saul seems to be having difficulty as of late. He never puts on his camera during our virtual lessons and he's doing less and less homework. He used to be a good class participant and well-liked by his peers, so I'm surprised he is struggling more than many of the other students in my class.'

Saul's trauma: Saul is suffering acutely because his social relationships and friendships were grounding him, and the lockdown and social isolation has cut off his lifeline. He has lost access to team sports and social gatherings, which are his main form of coping with stress. As an extrovert, he is really struggling. He is not a boy who replenishes through social media, and the world becoming virtual has left him feeling depressed and despondent. He feels hopeless and unable to cope. He is then left with his worries and has very few outlets. He feels unable to express his feelings because of the fear of being minimized as he knows everyone else is similarly affected. He does not want to be perceived as a 'cry baby' but he is genuinely not coping.

Interventions

Home: Saul is struggling in three main domains: social, sleep and school. For the social issue, his parents need to sit him down and plan how they can increase both his sports and socializing in a reasonable and safe way. Building sport into his day, every day, is key as exercise is not only a very good way to regulate our emotions but, for Saul, it is especially important for his social and physical needs. Activities like running, table tennis, long walks in nature, bike rides and hikes can be organized both with friends and family.

For sleep, he can be given some basic education about the circadian rhythm (which is detailed on page 106 of this book) and come up with a reasonable plan for modulating his exercise and sleep patterns. The key is for him to understand that sleep is also connected to his mood and this will impact his whole day. Oversleeping (not getting up early enough in the day) will actually directly impact his mood and energy levels, so see if you can 'experiment' with him just one week to see if the shift might help. If you can bring in a playful element, where you may be silly (come in playing silly songs or make his favourite childhood breakfast), this may make him more receptive and lighten the whole atmosphere.

For school, contact his tutor and make a plan. Ask for each teacher to contact him directly and set a virtual appointment with him, one-on-one. This appointment will serve as a check-in so that they can make a plan on how to help him. It is also a reminder that his teacher cares and Saul is the type of person who needs direct contact, not just in groups. Teachers are usually more than happy to add extra time for any student, but they can benefit from a parent who helps facilitate this. Of course, Saul is 15 years old and should be able to manage all of this on his own, but right now he is not coping and he needs your help. So if this appointment does not happen, his parents may need to intervene and help it happen.

As with other situations, if Saul does not allow his parents to help shift him, then having him try therapy might be another option so that he does not dip into the depression over which he is hovering. The fact that his normal supports are not being accessed is overwhelming to Saul and he needs help. If there is resistance to therapy (and there often is), suggest that they try it just once and see how it feels. Before the session, his parents could do their research and meet several therapists to see who might be the best fit for their child and then just make sure their child knows they can opt out. The therapist will often be happy to offer one or two sessions just as a trial and, without the pressure, the relationship can take off. Think about the gender, age and appeal of the therapist.

School: If you have tried to reach out to Saul unsuccessfully, then they can reach out to his parents instead. Too often secondary schools put all the burden on the young person because they are on their journey to independence. The problem with this thinking is that, when young people are suffering from trauma and not coping, they still need extra help. They do not yet have enough life experience to know what to do when they are feeling truly distressed. They need guidance to know how to develop their own coping toolbox that they can tap into as they get older.

When you get in touch with Saul's parents, attempt to include Saul as much as possible in whatever plans you make and then have as many of his educators get in touch with Saul. Although this seems effortful and time-consuming, you might prevent a much bigger issue in the medium term which will be much more time-consuming and sad. Being proactive and persistent (as Saul may reject first attempts) is likely to pay off and help him cope during this time so that he can become stronger, as he once was. As Saul had a lot of support until relatively recently, this time and effort may not last too long but doing it can prevent a deepening depression and de-schooling.

> **Discussion point**
>
> Discuss how the lockdown has impacted you. Everyone has had both negative and probably at least one positive experience. The positive may be well hidden for some, but search deeply within yourself. Name one negative and one positive. End on the positive.

Chapter 8: Divorce

Divorce: Daisy

Daisy's story: "My parents split up when I was a little kid but still argue all the time. They don't do it directly to each other, but through me. 'Daisy, tell your dad I won't agree to this', or, 'Daisy, text your mum that I don't agree to that'. They don't see the impact it has on me and I simply can't bear being used as a pawn between them anymore. They know they do it, but pretend they don't. Don't they get it? I've tried to keep out of their drama and explain I just can't do it anymore, but they just don't seem to get it. So, I look alright on the outside but no one knows how I feel. I worry all the time about others and I know I try to please everyone all the time. I don't really mind because I guess I am easy going, right? But why is it I feel so sad all the time? I feel alone and I am not sure who my friends are and who are not. When a boy likes me, I run away because I know there are so many cuter girls than me anyway and I know when he gets to know me he will just dump me. Anyway, let me put on my smile and just get on with it. When I get upset, I just cut myself a little on the top of my thigh as no one will ever see there and it feels just a bit better for a few minutes. I try to stop it because I know it is bad, but sometimes I just can't stop the thoughts and do it."

Home worries: "Daisy has always been a good daughter, she has always done her best at school and helps out a bit at home. Not enough, but you know teenagers! I did wonder why she blew up at me the other day when I asked her to contact her (dad/mum). She just flew off the handle and that's just not like Daisy at all. I guess when I think of it, she is staying in her room more and going out less. She just seems more angry and sad lately. Maybe it is pressure of sixth form getting to her? My problem is not with her but with her dad/mum. He/she drives me insane and will never support me in anything I want for her."

School's viewpoint: "Daisy, 16 years old, lives in both her mum and dad's home, I think. Joint custody, though surprisingly we don't hear much from either one of them. Daisy is a good student. She is predicted great grades for A-levels and she is not a problem at school at all. She is low key and attends her classes. I wish all my students were as well behaved as her! I have noticed lately that she has appeared a bit sadder, though. Nothing dramatic, but it's true, now that I think of it, she seems less participative and maybe just a bit sad looking. Maybe worth a chat to her after class sometime, come to think of it. Her grades have just started to slide a bit."

Daisy's trauma: Daisy, like so many young people with divorced parents, has suffered the trauma of divorce. To not own that this is traumatic to all parties is to minimize the impact. It is a very common phenomenon and we need to acknowledge in a non-judgmental way its strong potential for inducing trauma. Do divorces always lead to significant longer-term impacts of trauma? No, but a certain degree of fallout is universal.

I mention this not to have divorced parents feel judged, but so that we can be mindful that even though everyone is very aware of the impacts of divorce in the immediate time period after a separation, there is a longer impact on adolescents. Adolescents are developing not only their identity but also practicing for the first time romantic/love relationships with others.

In Daisy's case, it seems her parents have not managed to establish a consistent and safe communication style between them. They continue to include her and it is having a huge detrimental impact on her. Due to the fact they have done this for a long time, they are perhaps not even aware of the impact it has on Daisy. She feels like a pawn. This is unlikely to be her parents' intention.

The problem here is that Daisy has begun to internalize her parental discord. If you look at her 'symptoms', which include very poor self-esteem, insecure relationships with friends and an inability to explore relationships with peers romantically, they mimic the parental unhappiness. It is as if, by pushing down all discord and using Daisy as their mediator, her parents have unwittingly taught her to push down her own feelings and become introverted. Daisy is in touch with sadness much more than anger. Hence the feelings of depression. A problem here is that Daisy's sadness immobilizes her. Anger, at least, is energizing. So Daisy is stuck in her sadness and even in the moments where she expresses her anger towards her parents about being a 'pawn', she is not heard.

Self-harm

One way in which young people internalize their inner pain and express it is self-harm. Most young people I have worked with who have a history of self-harm will describe it as a way to numb the (emotional/psychological) pain. What they fail to realise is that it is only a very short-term solution as it provides only seconds of 'relief'. They can get hooked on the sense of control they feel along with the few minutes of distraction it offers. One cannot ignore the fact that the act of harming oneself is an inward expression of the hurt, pain, sadness and anger that cannot be expressed outwardly. This is a worry and the fact Daisy cuts herself on her inner thigh is more worrying than on her forearm where it is visible to all. She is hiding her self-mutilation, which, if seen, would be a cry for help.

Interventions

Home: Daisy's parents need to look underneath the thin exterior of pleasing others and work out a system where she is not trapped between them. She is calling out for help. She is not naturally a disruptive girl so her pleas are pretty low key and can be easily missed. Indeed, she lacks the energizing anger and the self-confidence to brashly demand changes, so they are easily overlooked. So, yes, her parents need to sort out the communication between them and honour Daisy's request. If not, she could slowly fall under the radar and disappear. It is very easy to imagine that, in time, she might decrease her school participation, her grades will drop, she will disengage with friendship groups and find herself isolated, and with very few resources to help her.

Another important note regarding 'over-pleasing' teenagers: Although it may be very pleasant for parents to have an over-pleasing adolescent, it is not always healthy. Let's be frank, an adult having contact with demanding teenagers is tiring, so over-pleasing young people can be a delight to be around. It is a real problem for girls in particular, as they are often societally (and often within families) groomed to "be nice" and "take care of other people's feelings". Though these are admirable qualities, they need to be balanced with assertiveness and a sense of self-worth, in which they learn to express their boundaries and needs. So here, Daisy's parents need to recognize Daisy expressing her needs and this will reinforce her sense of self-worth.

If you become aware of self-harm, especially in its hidden forms, it is time to seek the outside help of a therapist. There are many types of therapy. Talk therapy works well for many young people but there are also other forms such as play therapy (for younger adolescents), art therapy, music therapy, animal-led therapy, drama therapy and CBT. Research shows that the modality of therapy matters much less than the relationship established between the therapist and client. In other words, the relationship is the curative element in therapy, so go with whatever type most appeals to Daisy!

School: Daisy is easy to overlook. In fact, she is likely to be very typical of the type of teenager who is quietly struggling emotionally but because she does not demand attention through poor behaviours or with low grades, she will likely be invisible to most. If you are made aware of her poor self-esteem and self-harming, interventions that build self-esteem are key. In school, you have the opportunity to help her build on her natural skill set as she is academic.

You should start with her strengths and build from there. Perhaps pair Daisy up with a person who is academically weaker, but whose strengths are more social and compassionate. Make them "study buddies" or put them in a group activity together, so their contact is organic. Of course, if you are made aware of the self-harming, you need to contact her parents/safeguarding professional who will assess the best next steps, as hiding her self-harm is serious. It is not the same as a suicidal risk, as mentioned earlier, but it is very serious nevertheless.

Chapter 8: Divorce

> **Discussion point**
>
> Take a moment to think about the balance between your assertiveness and your desire to please others. If you were to put a percentage on what you are, what would it be? Now, put a percentage on what would you like to be? Finally, what 1-4 steps would you have to implement for yourself to bridge the 'present' you, to the 'wished for' you?
>
> For example, let us say you feel you are 30% assertive and 70% a pleaser of others, but you think you should be 50% in both, what would help you move from 30% to 50%? Step 1: Think very specifically about the language more assertive people use that would you be comfortable using. Step 2: Practice this language in at least two situations over the next week. Step 3: At the end of the week, check in with yourself and see how this feels. Does it feel different? Uncomfortable? Exciting? Empowering? Step 4: Reflect on how this assertiveness exercise has felt for you and decide on 1-3 new behaviours you can practice in the future which might let you shift your balance towards your 'wished for' self. Step 5: Practice!

Chapter 9: Loss of a loved one

Parental death/suicide: Lili

Lili's Story: "People think I am wild and crazy, and I guess I am. My teachers always tell me off for wearing make-up and wearing my skirt too short, but I don't care. Don't they realise that my life is crap and their telling me off means NOTHING to me? Sometimes I think that ending it all may be the only way to get out of my messy life, but then I think, nah, I want to live! People get fooled by my attitude and think I am a showoff, but if they only saw what I see inside. They call me a drama queen, but no one looks underneath. No one knows me and no one cares. They don't see the real me, I keep her tucked away inside."

Home worries: "Lili is a handful. School is constantly calling me in and I just don't know what to do with her. She's doing my head in. I try and talk to her over and over again, but she just doesn't listen. Well, that isn't true, she does listen when she is at home, but then it seems to go out of the window at school. She just needs to learn to follow the rules, like everyone else on this planet and get on with it. Last night I told her I'm fed up and she could go live with her Nan if she continues like this."

School's viewpoint: "Lili, 13 years old, lives with her mum. Her dad died a few years ago, from suicide, I think. She has a younger brother who seems like he is on track, but Lili is just one of those girls who manages to get under my skin every time! Boy, is she defiant! Does she not realize how tiring it is constantly asking her to just follow the simple school rules and focus on work? Why does everything need to be such a drama?

At this rate she'll get excluded as she keeps getting detention and her behaviours seem to be ramping up. By the end of the year, who knows where she will be?"

Lili's trauma: Lili has experienced the trauma of a parent dying from suicide and has not got over it. Young people who have parents/carers who die or abandon them are either literally or figuratively traumatised.

In Lili's case, her dad killed himself. It happened over five years ago, so it feels historical to others, and often this comes with the attitude among adults that Lili should "just get on with it". They may not articulate this, but this is the general societal message which they give out. There is huge societal pressure to put on "a brave face" and "just get on with it". People can miss the value of allowing time to genuinely address and heal their significant wounds. They are so good at putting on 'plasters' and moving on that they carry their wounds gently bleeding inside them all the time.

Lili was eight when her father died. She may have mourned it at the time, but at that age children still have a very abstract understanding of death. As a 13 year old, her father's death may have taken on a very different meaning in her life. She will likely question why he killed himself and she may have feelings of shame and guilt associated to this act. Also, the prolonged absence of a father figure will have different meaning for Lili now that she is an adolescent. She is suffering inside now, but people assume her grieving was done many years ago.

What is interesting is that if looked at from a different perspective, Lili is doing what society has reinforced – she is putting on a brave face. Distracting the world from her inner pain is just what she wants. It is just that she does it in a way we do not approve of.

As a therapist, I encounter these defiant young people all the time. Difficult as it may be to shift, I must confess I often feel a sense of relief to see a young person who is defiant as it shows a certain robustness, a resilience, in the face of great inner pain. It is often easier to shift such young people as they present as angry and defiant rather than sad.

Interventions

Home: Understand that, at 13 years old, the death of her dad will have different meaning for Lili than it did when it occurred at eight years old. Not only is she developing her own sense of identity and may be interested in others romantically for the first time, but she will also feel the absence of having a father compared to so many of her friends. Even if her friends are sensitive, she will feel isolated as she is likely to be the only one whose parent died by suicide. Lili is busy trying to fit in, like most of her peers, and she will be especially attuned to this absence. Also, feelings of shame and guilt will likely be present in how she feels about her father and his death.

Lili is likely to have a lot of anger and rage at the feelings of abandonment she is feeling. Where does that rage and anger get expressed? Perhaps she does not want to directly attack her sole living parent, but she is feeling it and power struggles are perhaps a safer way to express both her independence and her wish to gain control over something that feels out of control, such as rage and hurt.

So, Lili's mum should use her daughter's feistiness and inner strength and should not put herself in a power struggle with her. She should allow her some gains and allow her to express her independence, and she should support her in school by talking to educators and explain that Lili has issues of loss which are being triggered at the moment, and ask whether there can be reasonable compromises, as long as she also complies with her side of the bargain. Contracts with the school can be helpful, but only with Lili involved. She needs to be integral to all these discussions as that will let her know that the adults around her are hearing her and not just seeing her "poor" and "dramatic" behaviours and dismissing them as the superficial expressions of an out-of-control adolescent.

Young people of Lili's age are often very open to contracts and rewards. Build in rewards – not monetary ones, but ones that are more meaningful, such time spent between her and people she feels are supportive, such as with her mum or close friends and family. Contracts such as allowing her to choose which takeout food she wants, or helping her mum cook her chosen meal are meaningful and fun interventions her mum can try. Having her earn a fun outing with a friend or a special sleepover is another idea. Lili's mum needs to let her imagination flow and think with her, what are some fun things they can do together? This will lighten her up and help her reconnect to her inner child, which is lurking just underneath all that hurt, pain and loss of control.

School: Approach Lili's mum and find some time to meet with her and Lili. Rather than taking a punitive, detention approach, perhaps imagine what it might feel like to have a parent who died by suicide and the feelings of shame, guilt and lack of control this must bring. Combine this with the normal pressures of adolescence, and you may begin to understand and look at the message Lili is trying to communicate.

Applaud her for her good efforts. With playfulness, you can recognize her resilience and feistiness and help her find ways to redeploy her talents. Recognize her energy and strengths as they have helped her survive what must have felt, five years ago, unsurvivable and help her redirect them. Perhaps a drama group, being a buddy to a younger peer who is struggling as well, or being a class monitor, are all ways to give her self-confidence and redirect her more positively. Trial and error is called for, though, and educators should expect for it to not work the first or second time, but persistence and playfulness pays off!

Discussion point

For the adults, remind yourself what it was like for you when you were a teenager. Don't do this in a second of reflection but take 5 minutes and try to deeply reflect what it felt like when you were young. Ask yourself, how were struggling with your family (as every teen does) and how did you try to balance out peer acceptance, pressure and your own sense of identity? Remember how sad you felt at times? How out of control? How you experimented and "messed up." It is so difficult to allow our teens to make mistakes and not learn as fast as we want them to.

Chapter 9: Loss of a loved one

Bereavement of a close family member: Joe

Joe's story: "I cannot seem to get to sleep at night, I don't want to go to school, and I just don't feel like doing much of anything except play video games and watch YouTube. People don't get it, but my nan meant the world to me. I know lots of people have lost people and it's like I just have to get on with it, but I can't. I don't want to get out of bed, I feel like crap and I just don't know what the point of life is anymore. Anyway, I can't go to school as I worry what will happen to dad? He's all I have left. Not to sound dramatic, but I just wish people would just leave me alone and let me be."

Home worries: "Joe has never been trouble in the past but ever since my mum died he's seemed to withdraw from everything. I mean, Joe and his nan were always really close – she would take care of him a lot when I was at work when he was younger, but since she passed with Covid, he's not been able to move on. I mean, it's hard on everyone, but he's just shutting himself off in his room, eating half as much as he used to and refusing to go to school. I've asked his uncle to help out but he's refusing to talk to anyone. When I approach him he's not rude, just withdrawn and clingy. He used to be independent, full of creativity, taking photographs of landscapes and a happy-enough lad. Now, he says he cannot go to school as it makes him too anxious. I am at my wit's end and I don't know what to do."

School's viewpoint: "Joe, turning 17 years old in a week, lives alone with his dad. His mum passed away from cancer when he was an infant. Joe has always been a good student, but ever since the Covid lockdown and his grandmother dying, he's barely come back to school. We've talked to his dad a number of times and we're trying to be flexible but he's in Year 12 and he needs to get on with his A-level studying, otherwise he'll fall too far behind. I'm not sure what supports he has outside of school."

Joe's trauma: Joe is suffering from the trauma of losing his grandmother, who was an important support and family figure for him, but what makes it much more difficult for him is that it is triggering a past loss for him. Though he doesn't remember it, he lost his mother and he has internalised this loss. So, without realising it, his current loss not only carries acute emotional pain for him but is also triggering feelings that he may not have dealt with as they have to do with the loss of his mother. This explains why Joe is suffering from what looks like depression and is also very anxiously attached to his dad, as he worries that if he leaves home his father may disappear, like all the other important people have in his life. The fact that Covid took away his grandmother when he was not able to emotionally prepare himself, has triggered unresolved past grief and loss issues which he has never dealt with.

Interventions

Home: Both Joe and his dad could benefit from some family support at this time. Unbeknownst to his dad, the loss of Joe's grandmother has triggered some unresolved grief in his son. He may not be aware of this or even thinking about it as it happened such a long time ago. It is easy to forget because Joe does not even have a verbal memory of his mother. A therapist will be able to identify this fairly quickly and help father and son find a way to work through some of the attachment anxiety Joe feels towards him dad.

Joe is experiencing 'separation anxiety' regarding his dad, triggered by the recent loss of his grandmother. Joe may need a short-term medication intervention assessment by a psychiatrist if his depressive feelings do not lift after several months, to help him past the initial difficulty in coping. School might also be able to help if his dad contacts his form tutor and discusses ways to be flexible and come up with a short-term return to school plan which incrementally increases in time and commitment for Joe. Like in other case studies, Joe would need to commit and participate in this as well.

Planning a day trip together to take photographs, a past creative outlet for Joe, may also re-ignite a past support for Joe. He may need a period where his hand is held, so to speak, by his dad, even though it may not feel age-appropriate. It is only temporary and a concrete demonstration of how Joe can increase his own inner resilience again.

Slightly out of left field, but another idea is to jar Joe out of his feeling 'stuck' by leading (and having him join you) in an act of kindness towards a total stranger. Research by Sonya Lyubomirsky shows that one of the best ways to boost one's sense of happiness and resilience is to perform acts of kindness, volunteering, mentoring or expressing gratitude towards others. Joe's father could accompany Joe in these acts of kindness or activities and they can share the experience and how it feels.

School: Contact with Joe's dad is an essential first step. As mentioned above, a slow reintegration plan needs to be put in place that starts with what Joe is most enthusiastic about. Coming up with a visual timetable (every week building up time) and working back to a full timetable is one way you can suggest his return to school.

If this feels totally unmanageable, then discussions around dropping an A-level might be helpful. I'm surprised how rarely this is discussed with parents, as parents seem to think that the only route into university is having 3+ A-levels.

While it is true this is the most conventional and direct route, many universities have multiple routes including Foundation Years (year 0), apprenticeships and other alternatives which can be explored. While such an alternative might not be ideal, Joe and his dad would benefit from exploring all alternatives. Many parents and young people do not.

> **Discussion point**
>
> Challenge yourself to perform an act of kindness towards a random stranger this week. How does it feel?

Chapter 10: Fostering and adoption

Foster care: Loss of loved ones: Remy

Remy's story: "My mum is a crack head and my dad is in jail. My sister and I have been living with our foster carers for the past few months and even though they're ok, they are just not my mum, are they? I sneak off to see my mum, even though the social worker doesn't allow it, cuz what will happen to mum if I don't? I know no one gets it and she looks like a shit mum, but mum has a story too. Dad beat her up before he went to jail and mum at least stuck with us and protected us when he was around. No one gets it and when I'm 16 I'll go back and take care of her. I'd run away now, but I have to look out for my little sister. If I don't, who will? No one understands."

Home: "Remy is a good kid and so is his little sister. He bunks off school a lot and that is a problem, but I do understand what kind of pressure he is under. They came to us a little while ago and I think they are adjusting okay. I get the sense that Remy goes and visits his mum, though I'm not sure what to do about it. If I tell the social worker my suspicions, she'll come down hard on him and maybe us, too, but on the other hand, I have got to hand it to the lad, he just wants to do good by his mum and sister. School is driving me crazy with all their demands. Don't they get what Remy is dealing with here? How would they act, in his shoes? It all gets too much sometimes. All I hear is about his grades and GCSEs and this poor boy is just trying to make it day by day."

School's viewpoint: "Remy, 14 years old, just bunks off all the time and he will never pass his GCSEs at this rate. We know he has just moved to a foster home and they seem really on it, so that's good. I just wonder how we can help Remy to do better and come to class more? He's a nice enough kid when he shows up, but his attendance is abysmal. I just don't know how to get through to him and at this rate he will fail all his exams, except Design Technology which he seems to show some aptitude and talent for. In fact, I noticed that he is definitely an experiential learner and who knows how much literacy he has missed living in his home in the past? That's a lot to catch up on."

Remy's trauma: Remy comes from what is more obviously a deprived and traumatic background, having been exposed to domestic violence, drug addiction and a parent who is in prison. The trauma and worry that is less obvious to many is the ongoing worry which weighs on Remy's mind, centred around his mother and sister. He feels responsible for their wellbeing and likely doesn't share social workers' and society's condemnation of his mother's 'choices'. In addition, Remy has not had exposure to a positive male role model in his father, and yet he is really trying to avoid following in his footsteps. His attachment to his carers is nascent and he is likely to be wary of attaching too strongly, however good they are, as he feels loyal to his mum. In his mind, if he attaches strongly to his foster parents he is being disloyal to his mum who he loves and towards who he feels very protective.

Interventions

Home: Remy's carer appears to be truly curious and trying to explore Remy's dilemmas and how to best support him and his sister. She is in the very tricky situation of turning a blind eye to Remy's continued contact with his mother on the one hand, and fulfilling her protective role as Remy carer on the other, and her obligation to the social worker.

Ideally, Remy's carer, over time, will try to gain his trust and openly discuss the truth of whether or not he is seeing his mother, what is happening on these visits and how often they occur. It is also helpful to find out is how these visits are organized (are they propelled by frantic calls from mum or initiated by Remy?); is money being exchanged?; and what kind of interaction is actually occurring? One worry is that the environment mum is likely living in may have some dangerous elements for Remy.

Once the facts are better established, together with the trust and willingness of Remy, both the carer and Remy can together ask for a meeting with the social worker and ask for additional contact with Remy's mum under more planned and safe circumstances. The fact that Remy is 14 years old is tricky as he has a degree of independence (and, indeed, due to his past neglect will likely function as an adult in many practical ways), so to forbid him visits will only force him to go – you guessed it – 'underground'! Then the carer loses trust with Remy and the foster situation will likely fail.

Remy going underground is what everyone is trying to avoid. That Remy will be torn and committed to help his mum needs to be openly acknowledged and there needs to be a great effort made to give him sustained support in this area. To deny him what he feels morally compelled to do – to love and protect his mum and sister, which is a beautiful quality in Remy – will only force him to break the rules or to break his emotional commitment to his mother who, in his eyes, is a victim too.

So a balance needs to be struck between protecting Remy and protecting his values, and it his carer's role to help facilitate this. If they can manage this, they will be not only offering a wonderful role model to Remy, but it may be the first time Remy has actually experienced a parental figure who protects AND listens to him and his needs.

School: Remy needs the help of a mentor and could also benefit from a school counsellor. School needs to advocate for Remy as he has had a very difficult history and moving into a new care environment must be acknowledged as a traumatic transition, regardless of how wonderful his carers are.

Remy's carers could benefit from close contact with Remy's school supports, including his form tutor, mentors and such. Bringing in the family (including Remy) to create pragmatic ways to support him, making a visual timetable, and building in extra time for DT projects could be interventions the school employs to increase his attendance and sense of belonging at the school. The DT teacher could approach Remy and do an extra project with him, for example.

> **Discussion point**
>
> We often fall unwittingly into judgment. Even for those people who really attempt to be non-judgmental most of the time, it is natural and human to project our values and internal priorities onto others. Consider what you would do in Remy's place. Would you prioritise your family, carers, education, peers, fun, escapism, or just be confused like Remy, who tries to please many but ends up sabotaging himself? Can any of us really put ourselves in Remy's shoes? And if not, what is the best road to truly understanding Remy?

Adoption: Saskia

Saskia's Story: I was adopted when I was two years old and I have no brothers or sisters that I know of. I have never met my birth mum or birth dad, but I do know they did drugs and that is why I was taken away. The story goes that I was left alone a lot and not fed all the time so social workers took me away from my mum. I think my dad was not in the picture, or if he was, he wasn't around much. I have been living with my parents since I was two and I know they are good parents, but I just cannot explain this huge vacuum in my heart. My mum

(my adoptive mum) has been really good about letting me talk about my feelings to her, but I just don't want to hurt her with anything. My friends are nice and all that, but they just don't get it. Sometimes they make jokes that they think are funny, but they are just hurtful. I feel like no one really understands and I feel alone sometimes, but then I feel bad because, like my friends say, I have two parents who love me, so what am I complaining about? I know there are loads of kids worse off than me in this world, but I don't know, I just feel like a big hole in my heart and I cannot help but wonder if I had been a better kid, would my birth parents have kept me?"

Home worries: "We adopted Saskia when she was two years old. We couldn't have kids ourselves and we bless the day we got our little treasure! She is the centre of our life and I wish we could help her more because we see what a hard time she is having. Ever since she turned 14, she has just lost that joyous smile she had on her lips all the time! We have deep talks but sometimes I wonder if she needs another space. I have observed some tension between her and her friends lately and it is true that none of them are adopted, so maybe they cannot help her either? I worry about her but I'm not sure what to do to help as I don't want to bring it up all the time either. When she is sad it seems too hard on her to talk about it and when she is happy, I don't want to drag her down!"

School's viewpoint: "Saskia, 14 years old, is a single child who was adopted at two years old by her dad and mum. Not much is known about her past, although drugs and domestic violence are listed in her social work history. I have no complaints about Saskia. She is such a well-behaved young woman and works hard in class. She does look sad a lot of the time, however, but when I approach her she says all is fine. I've noticed she is less sociable as of late, but I am not sure what that is about. Many girls switch friends around at this age."

Saskia's trauma: Saskia was adopted at two years of age and experienced a fair degree of abuse and neglect in her home of origin. She has undoubtedly retained some trauma on a bodily level even though she has no memory of her first parents. Even though Saskia has found a loving and good family, she is experiencing a lot of grief, feelings of loss and questions around her identity related to her adoption. Saskia feels protective over her parents and does not want to wound them with her thoughts, but she does not have friends who share a similar history – this leaves a vacuum which she needs to fill. In addition, as the loss is pre-verbal, Saskia may not be aware of how profoundly she is affected and she could benefit from gentle and supportive exploration.

The age of the child when adopted will also have a significant impact on their struggle and issues of identity. In Chapter 12, we will discuss attachment styles, and Saskia's neglect and abuse during infancy will have affected her attachment. In general, the older the adoptee, the more issues around attachment there will be. Studies show that any child of two years and above, will likely carry more attachment issues. It is certain that regardless of how wonderful their home, all children who were adopted after two years are likely to have experienced an insecure attachment style which will be ingrained in them.

Interventions

Home: Saskia's parents want the best for her, and given her age, she would probably benefit from having a therapist or separate mentor with whom she could talk about her feelings without the worry of wounding them. Even though she used them in the past as her main emotional support, at 14 years old, she is searching for more (age appropriate) independence, and as her friends do not share a similar history, they are limited in what they can say to her. They also lack the life experience to contextualise her experience and to tell her that, as an adolescent, this is the perfect time to be searching and questioning her identity. As Saskia carries a wound, which is a sense of profound rejection from her birth parents, she needs a safe space to explore these feelings without judgment or concern for how her feelings may affect others.

Saskia is likely to want to explore how she may feel shame and guilt over her abandonment, and this is normal. Having a period of time where she may also reject her adoptive parents can also be normal. This could come out directly in language or through her behaviour. Part of adolescence is trying out new behaviours so to have an adolescent try things that are directly against the family ethos should come as no surprise. The key is for her parents to keep the channels of communication open so that Saskia can come to them at any time during her exploration and know she has a safe, unconditionally loving home with them forever.

Other than a therapist, there can be online or actual groups of teenagers who have also been adopted as a resource. Social media can be a good source of support here, although just be cautious when looking at sources due to predators and misinformation. Saskia's parents could also call the council to find out if such support groups exist in their area.

School: Educators can anticipate that there will be issues around identity at the age of 14 years for any child who has been adopted, regardless of their history and of where they now live. Obviously, the more traumatic the history, the more likely it is that the baggage will be significant.

Educators need to be sensitive and attuned to the adopted children in their class and should not make assumptions that they will somehow be unaffected if they are in a loving home. Being in a loving and secure home certainly mitigates a lot of the damage, but their beginnings will affect them regardless of their story. One of the most alienating struggles a young person who is adopted faces is that they can feel 'alone', as it is very likely that they are surrounded by peers who have biological families and, like it or not, society (in the form of films, social media and common beliefs) still promotes the idea that 'biological' families are 'better'.

Once the school has picked up on Saskia's inner turmoil, they need to help identify someone at the school who she can speak to once a week as a mentoring relationship. Building this support over time will give her a place at school to contain her worries and may provide some relief or signpost if she needs more help.

> **Discussion point**
>
> Imagine what it might feel like for Saskia to wonder if she had anything to do with her parents taking drugs or abandoning her? A 14-year-old mind can twist a lot of unknowns and blame themselves. How would this feel?

Part 2
Useful ideas and concepts

Chapter 11: Grief and loss

"Grieving is like breathing, but we act like we have to hold our breath. It is a natural process and if you pretend like you don't have to do it or that it doesn't exist, you'll end up choking or passing out." Dr. Shatavia Alexander Thomas

All traumas involve a form of loss and grieving, either directly or indirectly. In Joe's case, we can see a direct loss but if you think back to any of the traumas described in our case studies, you can see the theme of loss throughout. Loss and grief that you will never have a mother who is consistent and reliable; loss and grief of the inviolability of your body; loss and grief that you will never have the body you want, the school experience you deserve or the sense of confidence you desire.

Grief is the outward physical, emotional and psychological expression of loss. It can cause us immense suffering. Sometimes, a loss may not be direct, in the here and now, but can remind us of a past loss and this can trigger feelings in us which have not been dealt with from the past. Grief can deplete you of all energy, make the slightest task (such as brushing your teeth) feel insurmountable. Grief can manifest in many ways, not just sadness. Anger, guilt, anxiety, extreme fatigue, crying fits, dreams or nightmares, can all be manifestations of grief and loss.

When it is a person we have lost or have been abandoned by, we can be plagued with thoughts about how they could do that to you and why someone was so thoughtless. This can in turn bring on feelings of guilt and shame, because we feel unjust having these thoughts towards the one who is absent, but is it important to remember that are in fact perfectly normal.

Anticipatory versus traumatic grief when someone dies

Anticipatory grief is what happens before the person dies. It helps us prepare emotionally. It can allow us time to make amends, to forgive, and to say "I love you" one last time. It can help, but it can also lead to depression. It is what Joe did not have. In 'normal' times, Joe's grandmother would have had more time to say goodbye. In this instance, Joe's grandmother was taken ill, whisked into the hospital and isolated, and then she passed away. Joe and his dad were deprived of their hand-holding and hugs, which would have mediated the loss to a greater extent. Anticipatory grief symptoms can include depression, great anxiety about the dying person, and imagining what death will be like; in essence, getting 'ready'.

Traumatic grief occurs when the death is sudden, violent and/or unexpected. It can turn our world upside down. It can cause flashbacks which make us re-experience our loved one's death. The symptoms can include these anticipatory ones but also denial, loss of appetite and sleep, and loss of interest in daily life. Here, Joe is experiencing a prolonged period of grief in response to the speed and isolation that surrounded his nan's death. In addition, as mentioned above, Joe is additionally triggered as this loss has unconsciously re-opened an old wound which he has not dealt with until now.

Models of grief and loss

In order to better understand the impact of trauma on a young person, it helps to know about what stages we all have when grieving. There are a lot of models out there, but this section presents you with two interlinked ideas which might better equip you in your ability to help an adolescent who is grieving their loss.

Five stages of grieving: the Kubler-Ross model

Most of you will have heard about the five stages of grieving. Indeed, in 1969, Elisabeth Kubler-Ross, a Swiss-American psychiatrist, pioneered research on death and dying and delivered us this model, which is very well known. These five stages are:

- Denial
- Anger
- Bargaining
- Depression
- Acceptance

Kubler-Ross developed these five stages for people who were facing death themselves. Kubler-Ross's idea is that the dying person takes a journey that begins with denial and ends with acceptance. More recently, she and other theories have revised this. While the five stages are not so much in dispute, the order of the stages are. No longer do we see these stages as having a linear trajectory. Rather, we dip in and out of each of the stages in an organic manner.

The five stages of grief

- **Denial:** The reaction of disbelief and shock to the unimaginable, overwhelming news of the loss. It protects us as it delays reality and shock and allows us to digest the loss more slowly.
- **Anger:** The emotion of anger gives us the feeling we can fight against something. It is usually a temporary emotion but it allows us to pretend we have control over the situation or future. Unlike sadness, which is an 'immobilising' emotion, anger is actually an energizing emotion. The anger can be focused on a person (including the lost one), health care provider, a higher power (e.g. God) or the world in general. Anger protects us by delaying the feeling of sadness which might overwhelm us at first.

- **Bargaining:** Occurs when we try to think what can be done to turn the situation around. This is when we decide we will be a better friend, parent, spouse, or sibling. We might also devote ourselves to a meaningful cause and/or commit to living life more healthily. Though we are still trying to gain some control over the loss, we are often connecting with others in this process and this can be a huge source of comfort.
- **Depression:** This stage marks the profound sadness that is appropriate to the loss. It is when we are actually in touch with the full weight of the loss. This stage is often the most uncomfortable and is pretty much impossible to avoid, however painful. Symptoms like crying, losing interest in the outside world, poor sleep and reduced appetite are classic in this phase. During this phase, family members/friends are often uncomfortable and distressed for us and may seek to distract us. Finding the right balance between sadness and distraction is critical here, especially when the loss is profound.
- **Acceptance:** This stage is when we learn to carry on with our life, without that person, in the same way.

> **Discussion point**
>
> Did you notice that three of the five stages have a protective function that slows down the realization of the death so that it does not overwhelm us. Isn't the mind clever?

Continuing bond: Klass, Silverman & Nickman (1996)

An alternative interpretation of the Kubler-Ross model, called the 'continuing bond', was developed by Klass, Silverman and Nickman in 1996. The continuing bond concept posits that when a loved one dies, you slowly find ways to adjust and redefine your relationship with that person, allowing for a continued bond with them that will endure, in different ways and to varying degrees, throughout your life. In other words, you do NOT close that relationship. It simply evolves. You do not 'move on' or 'let go'. Rather it means finding a new and different relationship with the one who has died.

This concept disagrees with the notion of Kubler-Ross, which implies one has to 'let go' of the deceased or lost one. It also disputes that the five stages evolve in a linear fashion; rather, you can dip in and out of each stage.

So, if we go with this idea of a continuing bond, in what ways can we practically maintain this bond? I developed this image suggesting ways we can continue to have bonds with those we have lost, in death or otherwise.

Chapter 11: Grief and loss

Ways to continue bonds with loved ones

- Create a special place to write memories
- Use of their recipes
- Talk to them (out loud or in your head)
- Plan the anniversary
- Incorporate them in your special days (ok to leave an empty chair)
- Light a candle
- Finish a project they were working on
- Plant something in nature you can visit
- Watch old videos
- Live your life to make them proud
- Imagine advice they would have given you
- Talk about them to new friends
- Donate to a cause
- Give belongings as presents to other loved ones as gifts
- Write letters to the person you lost (keep or get rid)
- Take a trip they always wanted
- Keep photos or objects around
- Buy a gift that your loved one would have liked and give it to someone or charity

Discussion point

Look at the image above and identify what ways of maintaining a bond might appeal to you. What ways might you try and stay connected?

Throughout history, we see many terrible losses have led to incredible positive movements and ways of staying connected:

▶ In the USA, the loss of lives of teenagers to drunk driving (either as victims or perpetrators) gave rise to MADD (Mothers Against Drunk Driving), which actually led to legislative changes throughout the USA, Canada and Brazil. MADD started by the efforts of one single woman whose 13-year-old daughter was killed in California by a drunk driver in 1980.

▶ In the UK, the Lucy Faithfull Foundation was created by Ms. Faithfull who had a difficult and painful childhood. Her past trauma and feelings of loss linked to this childhood deprivation drove her to tirelessly work for protection and welfare of children. She was had a huge influence on the Children Act 1989 and earned her the nickname 'Lady Faithless' by a Tory whip, exasperated by her persuasive opposition to some government policies.

Grief pangs

Grief pangs are 'waves' of grief that are short, temporary, acute bouts of distress and yearning which can spin us into an existential and emotional sense of emptiness. They can last only a few minutes or for 30 minutes and be incredibly painful. That being said, although they are highly distressing, they serve an important function: they help us through denial because they fundamentally help us connect to our raw pain over the loss. This pang ultimately helps us connect and reunite us with our loved one in a different manner.

Complicated grief

Just a note about when grief tips into a more complex realm. Joe's grief, for example, would be considered 'complicated'.

For most people, grief distress can last from six months to up to two years. Two years is a long time! This is important to remember, however, as we live in a culture and society that wants and expects things to be over quickly. Sadly, our minds and bodies do not work this way.

That being said, the specific relationship that has been lost, and the context around it, will impact what one might consider 'reasonable' grief. I would suggest that if the acute grief last longer than six months it may be time to consult a professional to assess ways to help you. One of the key indicators of what many professionals will assess is how much of your daily functioning is being affected by the loss. If a person is not able to function reasonably well after six months of grief, then additional supports need to be put in place.

There are two types of complicated grief reactions:

- **Minimal grief reaction:** A grief pattern where the person has no or very few signs of distress or grief.
- **Chronic grief reaction:** Grief that lasts a long time, inhibits daily functioning, and its symptoms look like major depression/PTSD.

Both reactions are worrying. For example, if someone's parent has died and quickly asserts that "everything is okay", then this is worrying. Often this under-reaction occurs when a person had a complicated and difficult relationship with the person who died. When this person dies there is initially a sense of relief, but underlying it are unresolved sorrows, regrets and sadness. The person who is reacting with minimal grief will struggle to display any grief symptoms outwardly. Alternatively, the chronic grief can be exemplified by Joe. Joe's increasing isolation, inability to attend school and join in family activities are all worrying indicators.

Studies have shown that the following people are more likely to experience complicated grief:

- A person with already low self-esteem/sense of life who then experiences a sudden, traumatic death.
- A person who is emotionally dependent on the lost one and who generally deals with distress/stress by 'overthinking'.
- Men can have more health problems and depression after a partner's death – studies explain this is because men often lack strong support systems.
- Younger people who are bereaved often experience loss more acutely, but recuperate more quickly.
- People who lack of social supports generally have higher chances of difficulty coping with loss.

So, if you have lost someone and are facing complicated grief, how can you help yourself? The image below depicts some ideas which have been proven to help people through grief and loss. Please be mindful that if the person is experiencing any form of complicated grief, then a professional should be sought for advice and support.

How to help YOURSELF

- **Do not make major life changes,** if you can avoid it
- **Carry a self-help reminder.** Write down strategies like "go for a walk" or "phone my sister"
- **Take a positive from every day**
- **Learn to accept what has happened.** Acceptance is a big word. It is not "giving in" but it is coming to terms with how things are for now
- **Avoid self-medicating.** Excessive alcohol, caffeine
- **Pace yourself.** Slow down and do not expect too much from yourself for a while
- Gentle exercise
- **Ask for help from loved ones or good friends**
- **Have an easy story to tell.** With close people you might want more detail, but a stock story helps
- **Be involved with others.** SUPPORT, in person, online
- **Give yourself time to heal.** Weeks, months
- **Have a stress strategy!** Breathing, nature, music
- **Get into a routine.** To introduce a sense of stability

Discussion point

The list in the image is not exhaustive. Can you think of other ways you might be able to help yourself or get someone else to help themselves? Also, were there any surprises in this picture?

Some last notes about adolescents and loss of a loved one

How to tell an adolescent about a death:

▶ Make a safe space (meaning pay attention to the physical and emotional space when you tell them).
▶ Use age-appropriate language: clear, concise language and use terms like 'death', 'dying', and 'dead'. Do not us euphemisms such as 'passing away' or 'sleeping forever' as they are just confusing.
▶ Encourage questions.
▶ Be tolerant and don't personalize any response (including non-reaction, like not looking sad or impacted at all).

- Before telling them, consider how your reaction to the grief will affect the teen. Are you able to contain some of their reaction or are you too overwrought? If you are, then get someone to do it with you.
- Encourage them to share and not hide grief emotions/feelings.
- Expect the unexpected. You do not know how they will react.
- Be aware that while some teenagers might be comforted by having information on the five stages, others may not want to follow a 'rule book', and experience their grief as a lonely and individual one. While we look to this information and the stages as a guideline, we need to remember that our best role is as a LISTENER AND LEARNER, and let the teenager GUIDE AND TEACH us about their experience of grief.
- Stay away from saying there are right and wrong ways to grieve. Rather there are helpful and unhelpful ways to grieve.
- Explain that grief is ongoing but its character and intensity changes with time.
- Allow them to alternate between pushing you away and being clingy and anxious.

So, what now?

So far we have explored case studies of teens, trauma and the themes of grief and loss. We have explored helpful (and unhelpful) ways to interact with teens in distress. So, what next?

This next section focuses on attachment styles and your self-awareness. If you understand yourself more, you will not only uncover your blind spots and baggage, but also you awaken an inner curiosity which this book is hoping will get triggered in you if it was not already. This inner curiosity will not only aid you in our own life but will most definitely help you when you intervene with your adolescent.

Chapter 12: Attachment theory and styles

Attachment theory: Bowlby and Ainsworth

John Bowlby, a British psychologist, psychiatrist and psychoanalyst, was a pioneer in his field and changed a lot of fundamental thinking about children and their emotional development. In 1969, he noticed that many individuals who had lost their parents as babies in World War 2 had subsequently "failed to thrive" as adults. Indeed, many such babies died despite intensive nursing and medical care. Bowlby asked why, and the answers paved the way for his well-known and influential Attachment Theory.

Bowlby's theory posits that when born, every baby has the innate need to attach to an attachment figure (who is their primary carer). It does not matter who that carer is. In Bowlby's day, it was framed as the mother, but for our needs it can understood as any primary carer – be that the mother, father, grandparent, adoptive or foster parent.

The quality of care and attunement that this carer gives the child (mostly in the first two and half years of their life) will give the person a 'road map' for how they will interact with others and feel about themselves as adolescents and adults. This leads to each of us having an 'attachment style'. Everyone has a dominant way in which they attach to others, based on how they were cared for in the first few years of their lives.

In the 1970s, Bowlby joined forces with psychologist Mary Ainsworth. Ainsworth is well-known for her ground-breaking studies on the 'Strange Situation procedure'. Here, a stranger was introduced to an infant, and Ainsworth observed how the infant reacted and whether or not they were able to self-soothe once reunited with their mother. These studies led Ainsworth to conclude that there were three main styles of attachment: secure, anxious-avoidant, and anxious-resistant. Later, Main and Solomon (1986) described a fourth attachment style, called disorganised attachment.

The 'Good Enough Mother'

Donald Winnicott, a British paediatrician and psychoanalyst, developed the concept of the 'good enough mother' in 1953. This idea states that infants and children can thrive even if the mother (carer) is not a 'perfect' caregiver. More than this, he concluded that children actually benefit when their mothers fail, provided it is in manageable ways.

The key is in the phrase 'manageable'. This theory rejects the idea that the carer needs to be perfectly attuned. A perfectly attuned carer is someone who would anticipate exactly all the needs of the infant and respond faultlessly all the time. Obviously, such a caregiver does not exist. But more importantly, it would be unhelpful to the infant.

So, overall, a parent or carer's goal is to be emotionally, physically and environmentally present for their child most of the time, *but not all the time*. Temporary lapses are to be expected and not only can the child survive them, but they help to equip him or her for all the unpredictable twists and turns that life has in store. It builds resilience.

In other words, a perfect carer who was totally attuned to their infant would actually be unhelpful, as they would not prepare the child for many of life's challenges. We each need to develop the ability to self-soothe in order to manage stress when faced with disappointment, and build inner resilience in order to survive the journey ahead of us.

Combining these ideas, we can conclude that our primary carer gives us an internal template for how to attach to others as we grow up – in other words, a road map for future relationships. Bowlby and Ainsworth suggest that people have 'secure' or 'insecure' attachments to their caregivers which lead to these road maps. Basically, secure is when we have had 'good enough' caregiving; insecure is when we do not.

The four attachment styles

Attachment Styles

Secure

Insecure
▶ Avoidant
▶ Anxious
▶ Disorganised

There are four attachment styles. One is 'secure' and three are considered 'insecure'. What does this mean?

In the pages that follow, you will see a brief description of each style and I ask that you think of yourself first, before the teen you have in mind. Which attachment style resonates with you most? Understanding what style is dominant within us (as we all have traits that run across several styles) can help us with our own journey to self-awareness, which is fundamental in all our interactions with others.

Secure attachment style

SECURE "Being close is easy!"

Carers are attuned

Good non-verbal interaction with baby (touch, tone, facial expressions)

Baby learns that when she/he cries, they will get attention and needs met

Carers are consistent and available

This style of attachment is the result of consistent 'good enough' parenting, together with being raised in a non-traumatic environment. I am sure you can all imagine that there are certain situations which might impact even the most excellent and attuned parenting, through no fault of anyone, which can affect the child and their attachment style. A death, loss, war, environmental trauma or important life change can affect the environment and disrupt parenting, so that the young person feels insecure. If your environment and parenting, however, have been responsive and adequately attuned to your needs, then you will grow up with a dominant attachment style which is considered secure.

If you (or your teen) have a secure style of attachment, you are mostly able:

▶ To trust others easily.
▶ To have empathy (towards yourself and others).
▶ To feel confident when facing the unknown.
▶ To be self-aware.
▶ To accept your weaknesses as part of who you are.
▶ To learn from others/try new things, without feeling diminished.
▶ To react with less stress to stressful situations.

Chapter 12: Attachment theory and styles

Three types of insecure styles of attachment
1. Anxious
2. Avoidant
3. Disorganised

Insecure: anxious attachment style

INSECURE ANXIOUS: "I want to be close, but they do not want to be close to me!"

Carers are intrusive or ignore baby

Baby learns to cry and act distressed in hope for attention

Baby will likely be clingy

Carers are inconsistent

Baby has poor eye contact with carer and is agitated

Baby learns they cannot trust carer as they do not know what response they will get!

An anxious attachment style develops when parents/carers are regularly intrusive and inconsistent. By intrusive I mean they are **too attuned** to their child. Anxiety (usually well meaning) dominates their caregiving. These carers are inconsistent because they either overdo it or underdo it. Imagine how exhausting it must be to feel like you have to be *perfectly* attuned to your infant's constant demands for sleep, food and affection. As the parent is anxious, they attempt to fulfil these constant demands but cannot. When they cannot, due to exhaustion or (unconscious) resentment, this inconsistency is confusing to the infant.

This inconsistency combined with intrusiveness builds what is considered an anxious form of attachment and the child is likely to be clingy and perhaps befriends too easily. Teenagers with this attachment style are likely to be at risk of child exploitation, if we are not careful, as they seek attention wherever they see it. Similarly, they are also at risk of falling into problematic peer groups as they seek attention and are willing to compromise their values in order to 'fit in'.

A person with anxious attachment is often consumed with thoughts on how to re-establish closeness with their significant other (whether that is their close friend, partner, parent) regardless of reality. They might constantly worry, "I want to be close, but you do not want to be close to me!"

Insecure: avoidant attachment style

INSECURE AVOIDANT:
"Stop being so clingy and wanting too much!"

- Baby learns to mask feelings
- Baby may be detached from others
- Carers are regularly unavailable and distant
- Carers ignore baby's signs of distress
- Baby learns NOT to ask for help
- Baby learns to be self-reliant. Becomes a "little adult"

Avoidant attachment emerges in infants who are raised by parents/carers who are often emotionally and physically unavailable and distant. The infant learns to meet its own needs to the best of their ability and to mask their emotional needs because asking for help is not responded to. A young child with this style of attachment will be one that looks detached and does not attach to others in an intimate manner, and will have few, if any, intimate friends.

An adolescent or an adult with this attachment style may feel others are too clingy much of the time. They might say (or think), "Stop being so clingy and wanting so much!" This type of teen can have difficulty building strong attachments to peers and teachers. You may have tried, like with Daisy, but they just feel like they cannot bond to you, or to anyone.

These teens are likely to struggle to have meaningful friends hips. Often, they can be very well skilled and self-reliant as they have had to develop a lot of life skills due to their parent/carer being emotionally and physically unavailable during their younger years. These 'little adult' qualities can occasionally charm adults as they are often impressive, but be aware that they often mask a lot of emotional and developmental insecurities below.

Insecure: disorganised attachment style

> # INSECURE DISORGANISED:
> ## "It is hard for me to trust anyone really"
>
> Carers can be frightening
>
> **Baby learns to adapt all the time and is super aware of their surroundings**
>
> Baby is both frightened of carer but needs carer for closeness and safety so there is a dilemma
>
>
>
> Carers are the source of distress and often abusive
>
> **Baby learns NOT to ask for help**
>
> Baby learns to "dissociate" or separate themselves in their minds from carers
>
> **Baby learns not to trust and does not learn how to self-soothe**

A disorganised attachment style is probably the most worrisome of the insecure styles. It is linked to abusive parents/carers who have been sources of fear and distress for the infant/children. Here, the infant learns that the carers are frightening and struggle with their own needs for care, closeness and safety, with the unpredictability and fear that abuse and neglect brings. Teens such as Ellie or Remy are likely to have this type of attachment style. In more extreme cases, there are various ways the young person develops to 'numb' their pain (or dissociate).

As an infant/child, self-soothing is not taught and young people do not learn to trust easily. When you see this manifested in adolescents, you are faced with a young person who needs the most support, but they are often the most difficult to access and least likely to respond to you. They are not used to having genuine, well-intentioned support and care around them. They are the ones you will have to be very persistent with but, in time, you can form a trusting and meaningful relationship which can provide much-needed healing for them.

An introduction to the Attachment Style Quiz

In this next section, you are invited to take the Attachment Style Quiz to find out which is your dominant style. I have included this tool as (a) people often find quizzes fun; and (b) knowing your dominant attachment style can inform how you interact with others in a more self-aware manner.

In this spirit of self-exploration, when trying to help our adolescents, it is not only useful to know our own attachment styles as it helps us to understand our emotional baggage, but it may make us think when we overly identify or cannot relate to a teen. It may boil down to how we respond to a teen who has a similar or dissimilar style of attachment to ourselves.

If you have a dominant secure attachment style, for example, you might find it easier to have compassion for a young person, but if you have an insecure attachment style, you might struggle to relate or identify with the young person. This can be a great strength or weakness. If you can relate, then you will have a deep understanding and the young person may have an intuitive response and identification with you. This can be a huge strength and opportunity to build trust. However, beware!

Maintaining boundaries between your role as an adult and the young person is key, especially for educators (and also parents/carers), as they can become blurred. The teen is not a friend, they are your child or your pupil. Also, if you over identify, you can end up not hearing what the young person is actually saying as you are unconsciously projecting your experience/thoughts/feelings onto them, and not listening to what they are actually communicating.

So, if you would like, here is an Attachment Style Quiz for adults!

Just to preface, in 2014, Diane Poole Heller developed this quiz to help people discover their attachment style as an adult. There are many quizzes out there, but in my search for a good one, I liked Diane Poole Heller's quiz as it is serious but not overwhelming. It also has really thought provoking questions, which might help you gain a better understanding of attachment styles, so I encourage you to take it.

When you take the following quiz, ideally focus on your current or past partner, as the focus here is on adult relationships. This does not necessarily mean a romantic relationship but must be an individual with whom you feel the most connection. Who is your primary 'go to' person if you are sick or in trouble, want to celebrate, call with news, etc.?

In each section you will have a total. The section with the highest number will be your **dominant style**. You will likely have a mix of styles. Please note that this is not a diagnostic tool, but intended to increase our self-awareness and for self-exploration.

Chapter 12: Attachment theory and styles

ADULT Attachment QUIZ (Diane Poole Heller, 2014)

Secure attachment:

0= I disagree   **1=** I somewhat agree   **2=** I mostly agree   **3=** I strongly agree

Secure		0	1	2	3
1	I feel relaxed with my partner most of the time.				
2	I find it easy to flow between being close and connected with my partner to being on my own.				
3	If my partner and I hit a glitch, it is relatively easy for me to apologize, brainstorm a win-win solution, or repair the mis-attunement or disharmony.				
4	People are essentially good at heart.				
5	It is a priority to keep agreements with my partner.				
6	I attempt to discover and meet the needs of my partner whenever possible and I feel comfortable expressing my needs.				
7	I actively protect my partner from others and from harm and attempt to maintain safety in our relationship.				
8	I look at my partner with kindness and caring and look forward to our time together.				
9	I am comfortable being affectionate with my partner.				
10	I can keep secrets, protect my partner's privacy and respect boundaries.				
	Section total				

Anxious attachment:

0= I disagree   1= I somewhat agree   2= I mostly agree   3= I strongly agree

Anxious		0	1	2	3
1	I am always yearning for something or someone that I feel I cannot have and I am rarely feel satisfied.				
2	Sometimes I over-function, over adapt, over-accommodate others or over apologize for things I didn't do, in an attempt to stabilize connection.				
3	Over-focusing on others, I tend to lose myself in relationships.				
4	It is difficult for me to say NO or to set realistic boundaries.				
5	I chronically second-guess myself and sometimes wish I had said something differently.				
6	When I give more than I get, I often resent this and harbor a grudge. It is often difficult to receive love from my partner when they express it.				
7	It is difficult for me to be alone. If alone, I feel stressed, abandoned, hurt and/or angry.				
8	At the same time as I feel a deep wish to be close with my partner, I also have a paralyzing fear of losing the relationship.				
9	I want to be close with my partner but feel angry at my partner at the same time. After anxiously awaiting my partner's arrival, I end up picking fights.				
10	I often tend to 'merge' or lose myself in my partner and feel what they feel or want what they want.				
	Section total				

Chapter 12: Attachment theory and styles

Avoidant attachment:

0= I disagree   **1**= I somewhat agree   **2**= I mostly agree   **3**= I strongly agree

Avoidant		0	1	2	3
1	When my partner arrives home or approaches me I feel inexplicably stressed – especially when he or she wants to connect.				
2	I find myself minimizing the importance of close relationships in my life.				
3	I insist on self-reliance. I have difficulty reaching out when I need help and I do many of life's tasks or my hobbies alone.				
4	I sometimes feel superior in not needing others and wish others were more self-sufficient.				
5	I feel like my partner is always there but would often prefer to have my own space unless I invite the connection.				
6	Sometimes I prefer casual sex instead of a committed relationship.				
7	I usually prefer relationships with things or animals instead of people.				
8	I often find eye contact uncomfortable and particularly difficult to maintain.				
9	It is easier for me to think things through than to express myself emotionally.				
10	When I lose a relationship, at first I might experience separation elation and then become depressed.				
	Section total				

Disorganised attachment:

0= I disagree   1= I somewhat agree   2= I mostly agree   3= I strongly agree

Disorganised		0	1	2	3
1	When I reach a certain level of intimacy with my partner, I sometimes experience inexplicable fear.				
2	When presented with problems, I often feel stumped and that they are irresolvable.				
3	I have an exaggerated startle response when others approach me unexpectedly.				
4	My partner often comments or complains that I am controlling.				
5	I often expect the worst to happen in my relationship.				
6	Protection often feels out of reach. I struggle to feel safe with my partner.				
7	I have a hard time remembering and discussing feelings related to my past attachment situations. I disconnect, dissociate or get confused.				
8	Stuck in approach-avoidance patterns with my partner. I want closeness but am also afraid of the one I desire to be close with.				
9	My instinctive, active self-protective responses are often unavailable when possible danger is present, leaving me feeling immobilized, disconnected or gone.				
10	Because I am easily confused or disoriented, especially when stressed, it is important for my partner to keep arrangements simple and clear.				
	Section total				

Quiz results

You may now have a sense of your dominant attachment style. Let this inform you as to what your tendency is when stressed (and when faced with trauma). Knowing this about yourself enhances your self-awareness which is a core aim of this book.

Self-awareness is key to improving our interactions with our traumatised and tricky adolescents. Whereas there may be a lot of behaviours they exhibit, you will also be presenting reactions and responses to their behaviours based on your attachment style. Although you are now armed with a better understanding of your attachment style, it is not for you to then diagnose the adolescent but to enhance your compassion and deeper understanding of their challenges.

Is your past trauma and attachment style a life sentence?

Your beginnings absolutely matter. But are they life sentences?

No, they are not.

In fact, child and adolescent psychotherapist and author of *Nurturing Natures*, Graham Music, asserts: "Our attachment patterns are not life sentences but are normally quite constant" (Music, 2014). They are our road maps, so what can we do?

First, you are not alone. Research shows that about 40% of the general population has an insecure attachment style.

Having an insecure attachment style often means you have experienced some degree of trauma in your infancy. It also means that since your road map has more trauma associated with it, you are likely to get more triggered if a future traumatic experience occurs. As you are likely to have developed hypervigilance, like any other trauma victim, you are more sensitive to your environment and will often be more deeply affected by experiences that might feel traumatic.

A silver lining for trauma victims: Resilience

A silver lining for those who have gone through a lot of trauma is that, along with hypervigilance, you are also often more resilient. You may have heard the expression: 'What it doesn't kill you, makes you stronger'. This resonates with a lot of people who have survived trauma.

Resilience can be defined and has been talked about in a million different ways. Here, we mean your inner resources that allow you to both survive and bounce back from a very stressful event in your life. In this case, it makes sense that if you know you have survived a lot of stress in the past, you can survive more in the future. A lot of people who have had fewer challenges, may not know this and are likely to be more overwhelmed.

Resilience requires flexibility. Think of a bamboo stick bending back and forth in the wind. Like a bamboo stick, being resilient requires you to bend and adapt according to your environment. If we are to understand trauma in childhood, we can think of it as an *adaptive strategy which ensured survival* in their original care environment.

In other words, imagine an infant who is born into an environment which is not meeting their emotional and physical needs. In response to this, the resourceful infant adopts lots of adaptive behaviours (e.g., like being quiet, avoiding eye contact, not crying, or crying loud and clear to be heard). These behaviours are a positive adaptation to the environment because if they did not have these behaviours, then they would get neglected, abused or forgotten. Sometimes, they might not even survive. So, this infant grows up with these behaviours that are perfectly adapted to ensure they can emotionally and physically survive in their environment.

Roll on a few years…

It is only when this child goes to school or into their community outside this original home that they realise the behaviours that were so helpful for them in their original home, are no longer helpful at all! In fact, they are problematic.

Lili who has learned to be loud and brash, Ellie who has learned to be invisible, or Sam who has learned to defend himself by violence, are no longer functioning well in their current environments. These adolescents are confused because they became expert in their survival coping mechanisms and now they no longer work, and are in fact considered a problem.

I remember one client I worked with who was really insulted to be told that, given her history of abuse, she was likely less resilient than someone else who had not been subject to similar trauma. She was furious, and rightly so. In fact, she felt that she was highly resilient. Her abuse had been so violent and horrendous that she had barely (physically) survived, and to have gone through this meant she was a survivor in the truest sense of the word. Yes, it is true that her traumatic history's legacy was hypervigilance and anxiety, but inner resilience was there too, in spades.

Chapter 13: Trauma and our bodies

It would be remiss of me not to talk about our bodies in response to trauma. Again, the literature and internet are littered with information. Studies show not only how trauma impacts our brains, but also our entire bodies. Increasingly, interventions targeting trauma have bodies at the centre of them; like grounding techniques. Here are a few concepts that are not only easy to understand but can be shared with adolescents as they describe the relationship of our bodies with stress and trauma.

Window of Tolerance:

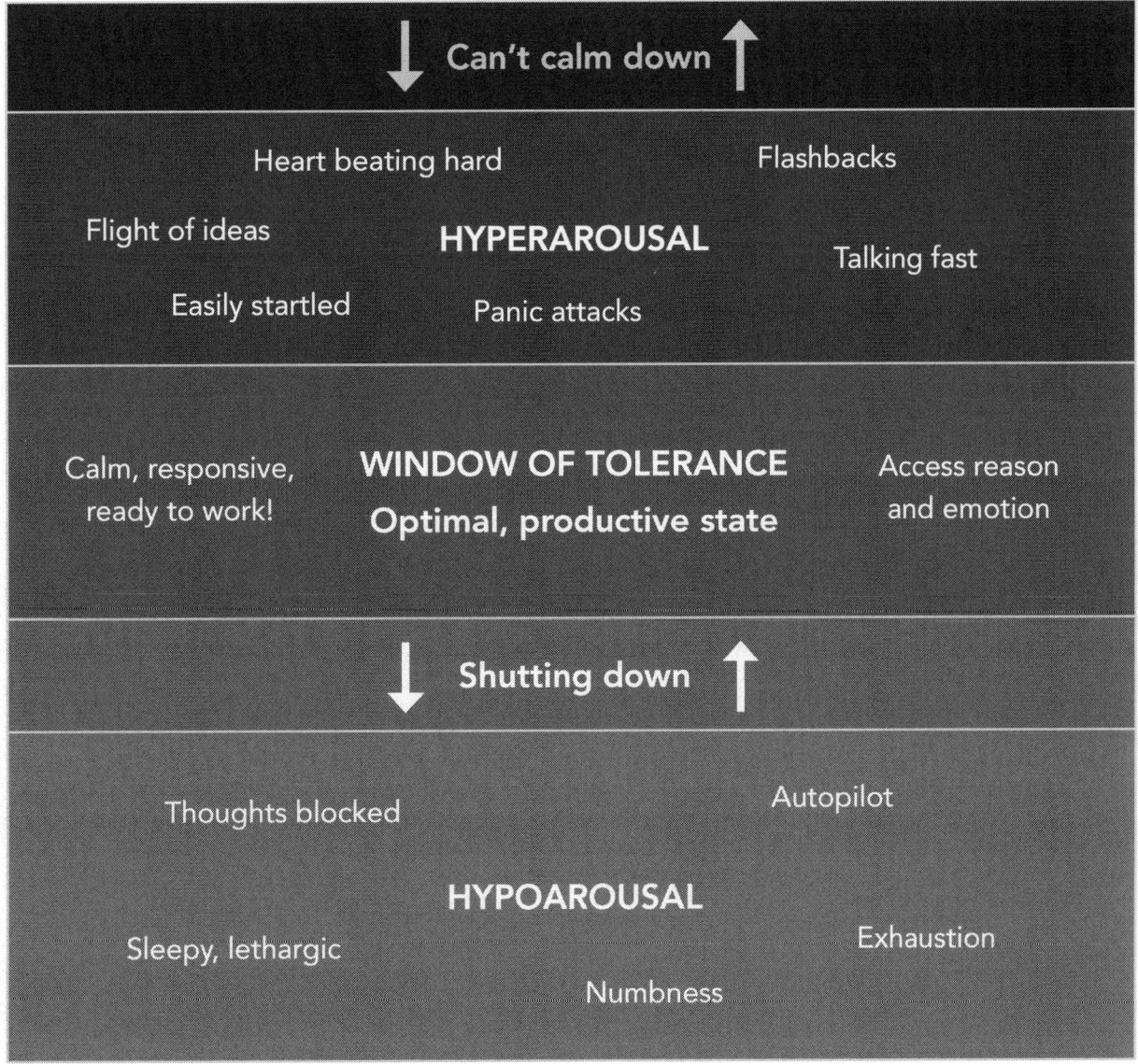

Trauma and Teens © Pavilion Publishing and Media Ltd and its licensors 2022.

The concept of the Window of Tolerance was coined by psychiatrist Dr. Dan Siegel. It describes a visual way we can take notice of our body and emotional states in response to different stressors. The optimal body and emotional state for each individual is when we can emotionally regulate ourselves in the face of stress or difficulty. If you look at the image above, we are happiest when we are in the middle 'responsive and productive state'. In this state we feel responsive, calm, alert, curious and playful rather than tired, anxious and defensive. The Window of Tolerance depicts where we work the most productively and where we are kindest to ourselves and others. We are not in a hypervigilant mode and we feel very present in our bodies and our minds. In today's 'mindful' way of thinking, we are non-judgmental and fully present to whatever we are doing and facing.

So, what do the other windows depict?

Hyperarousal corresponds to the mental and physical state we are in when we cannot calm down. Something has triggered our emotions, whether we are aware of it or not, and we notice our thoughts racing, our breath increasing, our palms sweating or any other symptoms of anxiety.

Hypoarousal is when you begin to shut down in face of a stressor. You may feel sleepy, detached, lethargic and shut down in a multitude of ways.

When faced with acute stress, notably in face of trauma, our bodies can go into survival mode and this triggers our amygdala (often referred to as the reptilian part of our brain, whose function is to protect us in face of danger) which can push us into a specific protective response. The hyperarousal and hypoarousal states are indicators to us that we are triggered and that we are no longer in our responsive, calm and productive state.

When faced with acute stress or trauma we will likely fall within one of these four responses, the **4 Fs**:

Flight   **Fight**   **Freeze**   **Fawn**

Please note this is not an exhaustive list, but these four are useful to know.

Before we get into their descriptions, it might be helpful to know that, in general, if you are hyperaroused you are likely to go to Flight or Fight. In general, if you are hypoaroused, you will go into Freeze or Fawn.

Many of us might have a 'go to' response (a bit like our attachment style), but again, we may vary according to the gravity of the stressor. For example, someone who might go into 'Flight' when faced with a fire in their home, might go into 'Fawn' when in their school, faced with bullies.

As with the attachment style, you are invited to think about your general response when reading about these four responses and then think about how this might play out in an adolescent faced with trauma.

Flight: fleeing from a threat

Flight is when a person runs away from a threat or stress. In the body, you are in the hyperaroused state and you may feel:

- Restless legs, feet, numbness in legs
- Anxiety, shallow breathing
- Wide, darting eyes
- Restlessness, fidgeting.
- Trapped or tense
- Sweaty palms, body
- Heart palpitations

Sometimes, when trauma survivors are still close to their trauma and have not healed, they can become stuck in this 'flight mode'.

Indicators that you are stuck in flight mode might include:

- Isolating yourself, focusing on perfection.
- Running away from attachments in life, moving from one activity to the next, being chronically busy.
- Over-worrying, obsessive thinking, over thinking.
- Being an 'adrenaline junkie', micromanaging things around you.

So, while the initial responses in flight mode are helpful, if you tip into the 'stuck' behaviours then you know you might need help.

This type of 'stuck' behaviour can manifest in young people who cannot settle into a peer group, who avoid your approaches or who immerse themselves in work or projects which actually push you away rather than include you. The key here is that underlying the behaviours there is a sense of avoidance, indeed flight, from truly helpful interventions which might help them tackle the trauma or threat.

Fight: becoming combative/argumentative when facing a threat

The fight response is where you fight back against what you perceive as the threat. This fight response can be physical and/or mental. Like flight, this response tends to be linked with the hyperarousal state as your body gets in touch with anger, which is an energizing emotion. Your body responses might include:

- Feeling trapped or tense.
- Clenching your fists, feeling a desire to punch, stomp to kick.
- A tight jaw, grinding teeth.
- Glaring or other aggressive eye contact.
- Knotted stomach, nausea, burning stomach.

Emotionally, your response range might include:

- Anger and rage.
- Homicidal and/or suicidal feelings.

Whereas a degree of this response can be helpful if actually faced with a threat, there are indicators which might show if we get stuck in this response mode, well beyond the point where the threat has passed.

Indicators that you are stuck in fight mode might include:

- Believing that power will guarantee the security and control you lack.
- Frequently feeling enraged and overly demanding.
- Being overly argumentative and socially isolated as a result.
- Getting into physical fights, without threat involved.

This fight response is a very common one among those young people who are troublesome at school and are characterized as 'troublemakers'. The responses they developed at home which may have helped them survive are no longer helpful when out of this environment. Often adolescents who come from tricky backgrounds are hypervigilant and misread social cues. They then come out 'guns blazing' and in fight mode to a (mis)perceived threat. This often leads to poor peer and adult relationships and can be a difficult pattern to break.

Freeze: shutting down your emotional and physical self in face of a threat

The freeze response is when you become numb or shut yourself down in face of a threat or high stress. This response is linked to the hypoarousal state where, in essence, you 'play dead' in face of the threat. It makes sense in face of a critical situation, but in my experience people who often go to this response are those who have a previous history of trauma and their body goes into an overwhelmed state. They shut down as they cannot find the energy to fight or run away. Again, a person will have developed this response in a situation where it might have been protective and ensured survival at a former time. Body and emotional responses for freeze might include:

- Feeling cold/frozen, numb, pale skin.
- Feeling stiff or heavy.
- Holding breath/restricted breathing.
- Sense of dread, pounding heart.
- Feeling the inability to move, literally, like being glued to the ground beneath you.
- Inability to get words or thoughts out, or to access memories.
- Falling asleep.
- Playing dead/limp.

Though this threat response is not a comfortable one for the person experiencing it, it can be protective. Though it can be helpful in the short term, people can adopt this stance in the longer term and get stuck in it.

Indicators that you are stuck in freeze mode might include:

- ▶ Drawing comfort in solitude and social isolation most of the time.
- ▶ Escape anxiety via daydreaming, oversleeping, getting lost in TV or some other form of 'spacing out'.
- ▶ Having difficulty making and acting on decisions

In adolescents, this can be manifested in those who are seen on the cusp or outside of social peer groups or locking themselves up in their bedrooms endlessly. They can look like they are wandering about and do not feel part of any social support network. They might have a disoriented and unfocused quality to their interactions and response and they can be somewhat 'invisible'. These are young people who are often not the overly worrying ones, but rather the ones on the periphery and it is only after a while their (physical/emotional) absence is noted. They fall between the cracks.

Fawn: Co-operating or submitting to a threat or captor

Many of you may have heard of the Stockholm Syndrome, which is the psychological coping mechanism coined by criminologist and psychiatrist Nils Bejerot in 1973 referring to the positive feelings some kidnapped victims develop towards their captors. Underlying this coping mechanism is the idea of 'fawning'.

The fawn response is when you to appease or placate the threat in order to get through it. This might include ingratiating yourself with a person who is threatening, and pleasing them. This can often be seen in domestically violent/abusive relationships where one of the partners seeks to appease the aggressor, rather than flee, fight or freeze. It can be linked to a more hypoaroused state as there is certain passivity, though it is different from freeze. In fawn, body responses might include:

- ▶ Collapsing.
- ▶ Playing dead.
- ▶ Acquiescing.
- ▶ Being super alert to the slightest change in the perceived threat.

Emotionally, it can include:

- ▶ Flattering the other person.
- ▶ Buying into a narrative that you are inadequate and/or deficient.
- ▶ Excessive caretaking or pleasing of the other person.

So, similar to the freeze response, this coping response is often uncomfortable for the 'victim'. It can help the traumatised person to cope in the short term but it becomes problematic when longer term.

Indicators that you are stuck in flight mode might include:

- ▶ Seeking safety by merging with the wishes, needs and demands of others.
- ▶ Giving up any needs or desires that might inconvenience or anger the other.
- ▶ Always saying 'yes' to requests.

- Making a habit over being conflict avoidant.
- Feels taken advantage of.

In adolescents, we can observe this coping mechanism when the young person seems to be subservient in their relationships or if they are the victim of bullying. In many instances, people who have histories of abuse have learned a lot of these fawning behaviours to appease their mis-attuned parent/carer. Like in other modes, while this may have been helpful in their environment of origin, it is unhelpful in others.

> **Discussion point**
>
> Imagine what stressor might force you to adopt any of the four F responses. Are there any that you feel you just cannot relate to?
>
> If that is the case, how would you feel if you saw someone use a response and you just cannot relate to it? For example, fawn is often misunderstood. People can see it as 'people pleasing' and, sometimes, frankly, a bit weak or 'pathetic'. However, it might have helped them survive something traumatic. Can you imagine how you might help someone who seems to be stuck in this mode? What would you do?

Part 3
Trauma Toolbox

Chapter 14: Working with PACE

The PACE Attitude

Dan Hughes, a brilliant clinical psychologist, developed the acronym PACE to describe the attitude we should all adopt when working with young people who have experienced trauma. Not only do I agree with this, but I think PACE is a wonderful attitude we can ALL bring to ourselves and to others in many of life's struggles.

So what is **PACE**?

PLAYFULNESS
ACCEPTANCE
CURIOSITY
EMPATHY

Think about these words. They are so simple, yet if we can really apply this approach to ourselves, and notably to adolescents who are struggling, it can really open doors for us.

A little challenge

Before I describe these words and what they might mean in this context, look at them and decide for yourself what each word means to you. Then apply each word to your attitude and think about ways you could apply each one in your relationship with yourself and with an adolescent.

What does PACE mean?

PLAYFULNESS is about creating an atmosphere or tone of lightness when you communicate with yourself and others. It means not berating yourself when you mess up. For example, most people have an inner critic which may 'tell you off' when you make a mistake, like calling yourself an 'idiot' when you make a faux pas.

The concept of playfulness means that we should catch ourselves when we are getting critical towards ourselves or others. Instead of the critic, replace it with a little playfulness in your tone or your message. Switch it up, and instead of scolding yourself, make a gentle playful remark to yourself like: 'Gosh, how many times do I need to make THIS mistake before I will get it?' The tone you use is critical here. It is not angry but light, silly and playful. A gentle tease.

Similarly with an adolescent, keep your tone light and accepting of them. Playful means having a light touch but it is very different from humour.

A word of caution: humour

When humour is directed at the adolescent and not at yourself, it has the potential to be misunderstood, especially by someone who has been traumatised. Gentle humour guided towards oneself, however, such as a gentle mocking and making fun of something you might have done incorrectly, can be helpful as it models to them that we are all imperfect. Adolescents who are traumatised often have a deep sense of shame and low self-esteem.

Making fun of the adolescent is therefore to be avoided. Don't risk it; banter can very quickly lead to misunderstanding!

Traumatised teens often judge themselves very harshly and their inner critic's voice is omnipresent. It may not look like it as it is often masked with ways to push you away, but it is there. Model playfulness for them, a gentler tone when you talk to yourself. Keep humour away from them directly because, being hypervigilant, they may misunderstand social cues and interpret them incorrectly. For example, making fun of an outfit, or a comment about their intelligence or appearance, even well meaning, might be misunderstood.

In addition, if your adolescent has an insecure attachment style, they will have absorbed a lot of mis-attuned cues from their families of origin. This increases the likelihood that they will misread you.

> **Discussion point**
>
> Did you know that studies show that a 'neutral face' is often misread by traumatised young people because they interpret it as angry or disinterested? Does this surprise you? This is interesting because a lot of professionals have been taught that looking neutral is good. Conversely, smiles are not often misinterpreted, but they need to come from a genuine place.

ACCEPTANCE is about actively communicating to yourself or the other that you accept their wishes, feelings, thoughts, urges, motives and perceptions without judgment. Now this can be hard! To be truly without judgment towards yourself and others is very challenging for most people.

For example, a teenager discloses to you that they are self-harming when dealing with a trauma. Most teenagers know that this is a 'bad' choice and a poor coping mechanism. Being lectured again and again is unlikely to change their minds and will probably close the channel of communication they have opened up to you.

So, rather than lecture them, listen to them. Really listen to them and hear what they are struggling with. They will likely be experiencing huge issues of shame, but they are unlikely to acknowledge this shame to you (or themselves). You can then acknowledge that their self-harm is understandable, given their trauma, but in the long run, frame it as 'unhelpful'. Then provide them with support. Help them or connect them with support that can help them explore other ways which are more helpful and less hurtful. The concept of 'unhelpful' coping mechanisms removes the shame they are probably feeling. You are not judging them, but rather accepting their urge as an understandable human response to an event that has hurt them profoundly. If you manage this, the adolescent will realise you are trying to understand them and this form of acceptance will help them feel supported rather than attacked. Change might actually happen!

> **Discussion point**
>
> In our journey to be more self-aware, are there things about yourself that you have difficulty accepting? Think of a fault you have. Recognise that we all have faults and that we are imperfect. Can you imagine actually having compassion and acceptance towards yourself with regard to this fault?
>
> Think about how hard this would be for a teenager who has never known acceptance at home. How would they have internalised this ability?

CURIOSITY is non-judgmental 'wondering' about the meaning behind a behaviour. To be curious in this context means to look, as a detective might, at what message is being communicated through the behaviour. To apply it to the example of self-harm above, the adult might genuinely enquire (in a gentle and light tone) what might have driven the adolescent to use this coping mechanism. Once you begin to unpick this and break down the problem areas into smaller bits, you might be able to make a more healthy coping plan with the adolescent. As you are not falling into the predictable 'grown-up' (intolerant and judgmental) ways of dealing with such problems, you may surprise the teen.

Curiosity can also be applied to yourself. When you see that you overreact to a situation or have a strong emotional response to an event or a person's actions, try to wonder why that might that be. We are often too certain about our own reactions and don't question our assumptions or our responses. When someone reacts too strongly it is usually a clue that they are triggered. For example, if you get disproportionately upset in a disagreement with your partner or child, perhaps it is justified, or perhaps it has triggered an old wound? If, let's say, you have been brought up in a home where your parents were emotionally distant and then your child or partner excludes you from a social event, you might misinterpret this and feel pushed away. Be curious about your reactions and responses: they are clues.

EMPATHY is when you deeply and genuinely connect with and try to understand and feel what another person is feeling. It emerges from your experience and imagination. Within the concept of empathy is a fundamental respect towards the other person and their experience.

Real compassion should feel challenging at times, as no one person has experienced everything under the sun and each person comes with their own story, strengths and weaknesses, which will both help and hinder how they negotiate any experience.

How adolescents with trauma react to true empathy, or compassion, is sometimes surprising. Intuitively, most adults think that if they are empathic it will be well received. With traumatised youth, sometimes this is not the case. Most adolescents respond to empathy but many will take time to trust it. If you had never had a truly empathic carer, how would you recognise and trust it later? This is why persistence and patience is so important when we interact with traumatised young people. The state of trauma demands that the young person is hypervigilant and that state, by its very nature, leads to mistrust.

Just like the other PACE elements, turning empathy towards yourself is also key in this journey. Being truly empathic – including being forgiving – towards yourself may be hard, as we are so often unforgiving. Using a playful, accepting and curious attitude and turning it inward can help us be kinder to ourselves and this will allow us to practice the 'muscle' of PACE so we an more easily apply it to others!

> **Discussion point**
>
> Think about the quote: 'Humans have the in built propensity to be GENEROUS, HELPFUL AND MORAL' (Music, 2014) What do you think about this? How does this fit in with the PACE model just described?
>
> One idea is that even if it is difficult, you should practice altruism and generosity towards others. Sometimes, PACE might require us to give the benefit of the doubt and be altruistic.
>
> According to a study reported by Moll (2005): 'Helping others fires reward circuits in our brains: it makes us feel good.' So what about that? We can feel better by helping others. When an adolescent who is clearly in distress makes you feel like you are at the end of your tether, perhaps just pushing yourself using PACE one more time, and persevering, might help?

Chapter 15: Self-regulation and grounding techniques

You may have heard the term 'self-regulation' and wondered what people really mean by this. Basically, it means the ways that we can contain (or not) our impulsivity and reactivity. Young people who have experienced trauma tend to have higher levels of impulsivity and reactivity which makes sense as they are hypervigilant and hyper-aware in their environment, as described in the chapter on attachment styles. Similarly, if you imagine the smaller window of tolerance of a traumatised teen, they experience triggers in their environment and may not know why they are acting impulsively or reacting in a volatile or self-destructive manner.

One of the keys to increasing your wellbeing (and this goes for us all) is to work on being less reactive and to think before we react. For this, we need to be able to regulate our bodies and minds in response to any situation that might cause us stress. A person who has experienced significant trauma will be less able to control their responses than someone who has not been traumatised. So, what can they do about it?

People come to me all the time for 'grounding techniques'. These techniques will help you return to your window of tolerance and I encourage you (or your teen) to try out as many of these as you can, in the spirit of playfulness! The reality is that trial and error is essential as all of these techniques work, but as an individual you might respond to some better than others, depending on your preferences, personality and situation.

I have separated these grounding techniques into two groups: Hyperarousal (for when you want to calm down and return to a more optimal state) and Hypoarousal (for when you want to increase your energy and come out from a numb, frozen or shut down state).

Hyperarousal techniques

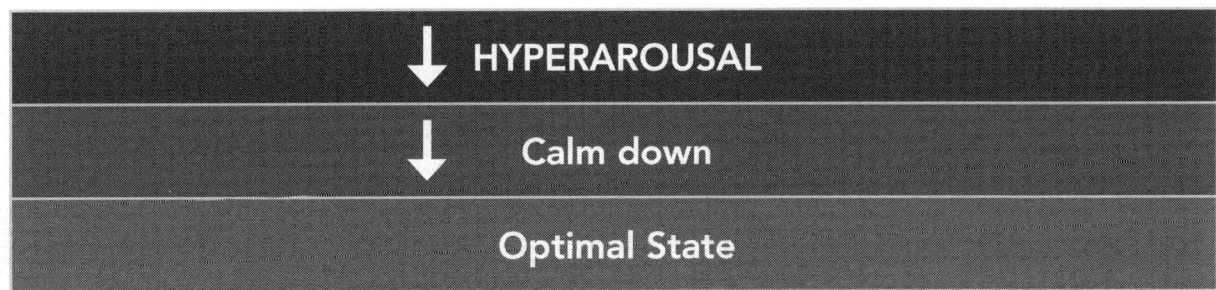

Movement	Breathing
▶ Do a task that soothes you, like cooking or singing. ▶ Throw a ball against a wall. ▶ Jump up and down. ▶ Shake/stomp off excess energy. ▶ Heavy lifting, pushing, pulling. You can incorporate these in your daily life, it doesn't have to be weights but any household item. Or lift a child!	▶ Slow, deep tummy breathing (imagine blowing up a balloon on the exhale breath and suck in a balloon on the inhale breath). ▶ Box Breath: imagine a box with 4 sides and you count up to 4 in your in and out breaths. Exhale (belly goes in) and inhale (belly goes out). ▶ Lie down, put something on your stomach and watch it go up and down. Link your breath to the up and down movement.

Playful

Singing and humming. This is why the 'om' in meditation works. It stimulates the vagus nerve and helps calm you.

Laughter is hugely underrated. Look at a comedy show, or meet a 'fun' friend.

Self-hug. Get into a comfortable position (lying or sitting) and wrap your arms under your armpits, on both sides. Then notice your breath and let yourself feel supported/contained.

Five Senses (touch, smell, sight, sound, taste)

- Drink from a straw (sucking grounds you).
- Put your hands in cold water. This is a clever way to divert your blood flow from your head to your hands.
- Heavy or weighted blankets help in the moment or at night. Deep pressure helps us to regulate ourselves.
- Take a cold shower.
- Move into colder air (inside or outside).
- Splash your face with cold water (once or twice). This is called the 'diving reflex' which lowers your heart rate.
- Drink a very cold drink.
- Listen to soothing music (remember what you find soothing may be calm or loud, e.g., many teens love angry, loud or and 'rageful' music and say it calms them down).
- Chewy food like toast or caramel/chewing gum.
- Chew or suck on an ice cube (with caution not to swallow, and not a technique for smaller children).
- Essential oils that soothe like lavender or sweet smells that trigger a positive memory, like cinnamon or rose.

5-4-3-2-1 Mindful exercise

Think of your five senses (touch, sight, smell, sound, taste) and try and come back to the present by locating some of these senses in your immediate surroundings. Look around you and try to identify:

- Five things you can touch.
- Four things you can see.
- Three things you can hear.
- Two things you can smell.
- One thing you can taste (which can be your lips, if you have nothing else around you.)

Hypoarousal techniques

Optimal State
↑ Waking body up
↑ HYPOAROUSAL

Five senses (touch, smell, sight, sound, taste)

- Drink something cold or chew ice (safely).
- Listen to active lively music.
- Smell essential oils: something sharp smelling, like citrusy or woody or mint (soap, scent, candle, herb).
- Suck a strong mint.
- Let a piece of ice melt in your hands, notice the sensations.
- Bite into a lemon/lime. This is a bit of a shock to your tongue, but it will bring you back to the moment.
- Eat crunchy food like carrots, cucumber or apples.
- Squeeze a tennis ball or massage it in your hand.
- Go for a walk in nature and notice the surroundings, touch a leaf, notice the texture, stop and actually smell a flower.
- Drink a cold or hot drink and notice the impact it has on your body.

Movement

- Gently sit on a rocking chair or bounce on a yoga ball.
- Dance.
- Sing loud and proud (in the car, shower, in your private space, outside in the fresh air).
- Yell and pound a pillow.
- Take a stick and hit a tree or the soil in the woods.
- Bounce a ball against a wall, vary the tempo and power.
- Stomp your feet, feel the energy go from your soles through your body.
- Star jumps.
- Run/jog.

Relationship/connection

- Ask someone to sit and complete a task with you.
- Share your feelings with someone you trust.
- Do an activity you enjoy with someone, like have a warm drink.
- Go for a walk with a friend/colleague.
- Connect with nature; even if it's only five minutes in the outdoors, immerse yourself in the fresh air.
- Call a friend or loved one.
- Hold someone's hand.
- Ask for a hug from someone you care about.
- Listen to music that connects you to a person or a memory which means something to you.
- Self-hug. Get into a comfortable position (lying or sitting) and wrap your arms under your armpits, on both sides. Then notice your breath and let yourself feel supported/contained.
- Hug or play with your pet

Please feel free to experiment and see how you respond to some of these techniques. Try them out. These grounding techniques will help you 'in the moment' to regulate yourself when you are stressed. If you practice a technique alongside a teen, this removes the notion that *they* have 'the problem'. And it can be fun! If we can connect with some lightness in moments of difficulty, this can begin to shift us away from the mood and feelings that overwhelm us.

Please remember to experiment at least three or four times with any technique before you discount it as ineffective as they take time to ingrain. Again, many of these techniques lend themselves to the spirit of playfulness and curiosity, both of which are such important elements of the PACE attitude. The more we practice, the more natural it can feel.

Chapter 16: The importance of self-care

This chapter discusses aspects of self-care that are crucial to you and your teen's sense of wellbeing. In contrast to the grounding techniques explored in the last chapter, this chapter illustrates on-going strategies and goals we can set ourselves that have a longer-term impact on our lives. Self-care involves lifelong commitments that can augment and wane depending on our lives, while grounding techniques can help us in the moment.

One key point about self-care: please **do not decrease** self-care when overwhelmed, you actually need to **increase it**. It is natural for people to put self-care aside when they feel stressed. Please do not do this, even though instinctively we all decide we are 'too busy' or overwhelmed to engage in self-care when distressed. We must instead encourage as much self-care in our daily routines as possible, and boost them when stressors come into our lives. Become role models for your family and/or students and help them to identify their self-care gaps and remedies. You may literally have to hold the hand of a teen and lead them by example. Accompany them in increasing self-care: I can assure you, you will benefit from it as well.

One way to increase self-care is to use the concept of seven pillars of wellbeing: emotional, spiritual (not necessarily to be confused with religious), physical, social, occupational, environmental and intellectual. The idea is that we all need to create a balance and a decent level of self-care in each of these domains.

With regard to these seven pillars, I have developed a worksheet for teenagers which you can use:

Chapter 16: The importance of self-care

Seven Pillars of Wellbeing

Mentee name

....

Date

....

Emotional

I manage my stress (on a scale of 1-5)

-0 ———————————————— 5+

I feel confident...

-0 ———————————————— 5+

Spiritual

I feel like I have purpose in my life

-0 ———————————————— 5+

I feel passionate about something

-0 ———————————————— 5+

Physical

I eat healthily

-0 ———————————————— 5+

I have a good balance of exercise and sleep

-0 ———————————————— 5+

Social

I feel connected to my family

-0 ———————————————— 5+

I feel supported by my friends

-0 ———————————————— 5+

Occupational

I know what my next steps are to pursue: Educational/Job

-0 ———————————————— 5+

My dream job in the future

-0 ———————————————— 5+

Environmental

I feel safe at home/work/school

-0 ———————————————— 5+

I feel empowered to speak my mind

-0 ———————————————— 5+

Intellectual

I have a plan for my future

-0 ———————————————— 5+

I feel content with the skills and hobbies I have

-0 ———————————————— 5+

If I could pick 3 areas I want to work on with my mentor (from the above) what are they.

....

Signature ....

The best way to use this worksheet is to ask the teen to fill it out alongside you (you can also fill out your own, as it is not age-specific) and rate themselves between 0-5. Five means they are supremely happy with this area of wellbeing and zero means they have no tools to self-soothe in this area at all.

This worksheet can be helpful as it can help you and your teen identify where they are struggling or have imbalance in their lives. In response to this, you can then also target the 'weaker' areas to help them strengthen their sense of wellbeing and resilience. Once you have unpicked the areas of low scores, you can see the areas that self-care activities may target. Try and choose two areas that are troublesome and commit yourself (make a promise to yourself or each other) that you will do one thing a day from the list you have made.

Below is a box of ideas that can target each pillar: they are just suggestions and are not exhaustive. Try and make your own self-care list with your teen. The key is regularity and repetition of the activity. Commit to one self-care activity a day. Remember, when stressed, we need to increase, not decrease, self-care.

Pillars of wellbeing	Possible self-care activities
Emotional	▶ Go out for coffee/tea with a friend. ▶ Go for a walk with a friend. ▶ Write in a journal. ▶ Watch cheesy shows that make you laugh. ▶ Spend quality time with loved ones. ▶ Contact an old friend you forgot about. ▶ Watch something sad and let yourself cry. ▶ Re-read a book you loved or re-watch a movie you love. ▶ Sing (alone, if you are shy). ▶ Listen to music and let the music affect your body.
Spiritual	▶ Read something short or long that inspires you. ▶ Go for a walk or hike in nature. ▶ Make a list of aspirations and take one step towards your goal. ▶ Sing/pray/meditate/try mindfulness. ▶ Pick a symbol that represents you and draw it or get one and put it in your room next to your bed.
Physical	▶ Think and commit to a sport or activity that uses your body and do it two or three times a week. ▶ Slow down when you eat your next treat and really savour it. Notice the texture, taste, smoothness, sweetness, saltiness. ▶ Sing/dance/play/walk/run/skip. ▶ Try a new recipe once a week that is healthy, and take your time with it. ▶ Try to commit to a regular, healthy diet and drink loads of water.
Social	▶ Book an outing with a friend. ▶ Reach out to someone you have not contacted in a while. ▶ Have a fun evening out with a friend. ▶ Try a new group with an interest you might have. →

Pillars of wellbeing	Possible self-care activities
Occupational	▶ Listen to an interesting podcast or educational programme. ▶ Learn a new skill. ▶ Try a new hobby. ▶ Try and meet a new person who does something that interests you and ask them about it.
Environmental	▶ Try and make a safe place somewhere in your home and make it peaceful to you. ▶ If you are stressed, carry something small in your pocket as a symbol of someone you love. ▶ Take a risk and speak out to someone you trust, and tell them a feeling that you wouldn't usually express.
Intellectual	▶ Try to learn something new. ▶ Ask someone you admire about their journey and how they got to where they are. ▶ Go to see a new film or visit a museum. ▶ Set yourself a new goal related to one of your dreams.

Sleep and nutrition

It would be remiss of me not to mention the importance of sleep and nutrition for anyone suffering trauma, and this is particularly important for teens. Both sleep and nutrition are important forms of self-care, and they can present a particular challenge for most teenagers as parents/carers often report their teens oversleep, suffer from insomnia (often aided by the blue light of phones and tablets) and eat a lot of 'rubbish' junk food with their peers (even if this is not available at home).

Sleep

There is more and more research that shows an important link between sleep and mood. So if your teen suffers from symptoms of depression or low mood, regulating sleep may be a very helpful intervention. Adherence to our Circadian rhythms (as much as possible) will not only positively impact their mood but will tap into energy they may not have felt they had.

Circadian rhythms are physical, mental and behavioural changes that follow a 24-hour cycle. When we disrupt these cycles, problems occur. We have not evolved yet to overcome this basic programming, and though it is no one's fault, going to bed very late and waking up late impacts negatively on our mood, levels of energy and productivity.

So how can you talk about it to your teen?

Sharing the science (in a chatty and curious manner) can help, as young people may be more open to simple concepts that are not 'moral' arguments, as they know they need to sleep and wake up earlier, they just find it very difficult to do so.

Chapter 16: The importance of self-care

Below is an image that may be helpful to share with your teen as it is clear and shows how the chemicals in our body function:

Discussion point

Perhaps imagine your current sleep pattern and your daily routines, and work out if you are actually following your body's natural strengths. Did you know you are most alert in the late morning or most coordinated after noon? Did you realise that the reason the blue light of computers and phones is so discouraged late at night is not only due to information overload, but that it actually disrupts production of your melatonin (a hormone that helps you sleep)? So when research says to turn off phones at least an hour or two before bedtime, it is not just for teenagers, but everyone. Is your whole household prepared to experiment with this?

Did you realise that sleeping in on weekends actually impacts on your sleep as much as going to bed late? Can you possibly show your teen this cycle and explain that it is science, and not you as the parent/carer, which tells us all what works best for sleep?

Another discussion point

Before we move onto nutrition, encourage your teenager to experiment with forcing themselves to wake up earlier (any time before 9am), and to try it for a week and see how this affects their fatigue and energy levels. Is their mood better (after the first couple days of grumpiness)? Reward them with accolades and maybe even privileges if they can sustain this. It should impact on their mood beneficially and, although terribly difficult, it may help them with school and generally how they cope with ordinary stressors in life.

Chapter 16: The importance of self-care

Nutrition

In terms of nutrition, we all know that junk food is bad for you. The question is what to do about it.

Rather than focus on the weight aspect, which is so pervasive in our society, there is interesting research and a lot of information available on the internet about trauma and gut health. Increasingly, it is accepted that junk food is not only impactful on your body and its health, but also affects how trauma is processed and that actually eating a lot of sugars, salts and manufactured chemicals in our processed foods shuts down and affects our bodies, and this affects our mood directly.

Educating yourself and your teen is important here. The way in which you learn about and tackle these issues needs to stay away from descending into a 'power struggles' between the two of you, as there needs to also be an acceptance in the adults that, for the moment, a lot of teens will have enormous pressure to join their peers in binge eating and group outings to junk food establishments. Until our society actually begins to make healthy foods more attractive, available and affordable to young people, the reality is that most teens will indulge in a certain amount of junk food.

So what do we do? One approach is to embrace learning together about the impacts of unhealthy (though often tasty, let's acknowledge this) food and how it feels in the body.

> **Discussion point**
>
> Here is a family challenge: within your family unit, experiment and have different nights on which you can explore healthy options and see how each person sleeps, feels (their mood and energy) and is satiated. Maybe for the real pioneers, try an unhealthy, junk food night and apply the same exploration to this and notice how everyone responds. Bring a scientific (non-judgmental and fact-finding) approach and also discuss openly how it must be difficult for the teen to accompany their friends to junk and fast food establishments and then not join in.

Perhaps there needs to be an acceptance that there will be a certain amount of junk food indulgence, but this needs to be balanced out at home where our guts can get used to less processed, healthier foods.

Teens want to fit in and it can be also quite alienating, unless their social peer group norms embrace it, to withstand the pressure. Most cannot. Many of us have to accept that even if we model healthy eating and provide healthy food most of the time, there will be a time in adolescence (between 13 and 16 in my experience) where the pressure to follow peers will lead to expressions of independence that sometimes go against family wishes and norms. Again, keeping the channels of communication open and holding the family line of 'healthy food most of the time, with a few exceptions', will broaden the young person's awareness so that when they are genuinely more independent as young adults, they can choose healthier options themselves.

It is important to have plenty of healthy snacks around and make them as appealing as possible. Young people like to have snacks for when friends come over so having healthier options that are not deemed too boring can help. If you are inclined, having homemade biscuits, cakes and other snacks can also help reduce unwanted additives, salts and sugars that exist in junk food.

Lastly, Vitamins D and B are reported to help support a healthy gut and sleep, as well as probiotic kefir and other yogurts. These probiotic foods and vitamins can help supply your gut with much improved gut 'flora', which basically means good bacteria that helps with digestion and improved sleep. Magnesium, a natural supplement, taken before bedtime can also help balance nutrition and has been linked to a safe way to improve sleep quality by activating the neurotransmitters and helping calm the body and mind.

Chapter 17: Key strategies for parents and carers

As we come to the conclusion of this book, my hope is that many of you will not treat this as a 'trauma bible', but rather that you have found it stimulating and that it has helped you reflect on yourself and the adolescents in your life. The key to adopting a genuine, non-judgmental, curious, playful and empathic tone with our teens lies in our working alongside them, rather than in front (dictating) or behind (pushing) them.

I hope you find these last few suggestions of strategies and interventions helpful as you become the **detective, partner and supporter of your traumatised teen**.

- **Translate, don't educate.** When our adolescents are stressed, they need support from us as parents first, and guidance later. It is a difficult task, as sometimes the defiance and breaking of family norms can be terrifying. The problem is that, if your adolescent does not genuinely see you as accepting and curious of what underlies their behaviours, then they will go underground and just do those behaviours behind your back. To re-establish their trust in you after this is much more onerous and can quickly build a great divide between you and them.
- **Actively link up with schools/educators.** As the young person gets older, they will experience increasing pressure to be independent. While this is wonderful when the teen is not in distress, it is a real missed opportunity if you do not work closely with the school. There will be at least one person at school who your teen has warmed up to; find them and work with them. Adolescents need to be 'held' with as many hands as possible as it makes them feel safe when they are feeling unsafe, internally.
- **Golden 'talk time' with teens tends to be at bedtime.** This is a difficult one for most parents who often look forward to some time off in the evening to decompress after a long day of parenting and work. Teens tend to think at night. They are isolated with their thoughts, they are laying in bed, and this is the time they often are the most vulnerable and are open to meaningful chats. So, as a parent, combat your urge (which is perfectly normal) to move the chat to the next day, or end it quickly, as this is golden bonding time. Although it might be hard when you're tired, remember that this effort now might very well pay off and avert many more troubling days and nights to come.
- **Limit access to digital phones, computers and TV at night.** In balance with the compassion you give, having some limits is critical too. Especially with younger teens (ages 11-14), helping them by enforcing rules around screen time will help them disconnect and sleep. It is also important to agree with them that school nights

are different to weekends and holidays. Sleep is so tricky for many teens, so the use of music and books can be helpful.

- **Power of PACE.** Playfulness, Acceptance, Curiosity and Empathy are key to developing a better relationship with your adolescent.
- **Expect rejection.** Most adolescents will reject or push you away if you are trying to build a bridge with them, especially if this departs from your previous relationship with them.
- **Persist and it will pay off.** You may have to persist quietly and with subtle gestures rather than directly, but it will help heal the adolescent. For example, if your adolescent refuses to let you attend an important meeting (with the doctor or school for example), do not insist. Give them an object, a supportive text or a little note that they will discover en route, so that they know you are accompanying them in spirit.
- **Unconditional acceptance.** This is different from unconditional love. It is the ability to truly listen and work through any issue with your teen, side by side.
- **Combat the natural fear when you are practicing curiosity.** It is natural to not want to know if your child is self-harming, having suicidal ideation, taking drugs or sleeping around. It is painful to find out and most of us will pull away or delay these conversations. Please fight this urge. The problem does not go away, and in fact simply goes underground.
- **Get support for yourself.** This support might be in the moment or more long-term. If you need a friend or partner to help you with difficult conversations about self-harm, suicide, drugs, sex, sexuality or any other high-risk behaviour, ask. You may also need professional support or support groups. Reach out online, to the school, to your community, or to spiritual guides.
- **Practice acts of kindness.** Try and explore this and model it, or accompany your teen in practicing random acts of kindness and see how it feels afterwards. It is linked to a higher sense of wellbeing, so try it!
- **Frame high-risk behaviours as 'unhelpful' as opposed to 'bad'.** In your efforts to discuss a worrying or high-risk behaviour, use language that characterises the behaviours as 'unhelpful' though understandable in their context. Then help your teen to, in time, develop more 'helpful' behaviours to replace the unhelpful ones.
- **Be a listener and learner of your adolescent.** Let them guide and teach you about what they are truly feeling and what underlies their worrying behaviour.
- **Develop and role model your 'observer's' voice rather than a 'self-critical' voice.** Use yourself as a model to show your adolescent that you are also struggling at times. Show them through example that you are also on a journey of self-awareness. Try to model playfulness and empathy towards yourself.
- **Do not use euphemisms when talking about difficult subjects.** When talking about self-harm, suicide, loss and death, use the appropriate language and be clear and concise. Other language is confusing.
- **Listen to the question your teen is asking and do not answer more (or less).** This skill is a difficult one for many adults as we tend to project our own experiences onto teens. For example, if your teen reveals to you that they have been exposed to pornography or inappropriate social media, remember their age. Remember that a 12 year old's understanding and experience of sex, context, relationships and

intimacy will be very different from a 16 year old's. Indeed, a protected 12 year old might have very little notion of what sex looks like and they way they will register the images will be different to an adult.

▶ **Invite and create a space in your home for your teen and their friends to hang out.** Particularly if your teen is struggling with communicating with you, try and create a space where your teen can welcome and 'hang' with their friends on a weekly basis. This may mean sleepovers and a sacrifice in terms of your privacy and quiet, but it is useful to assess what type of friends your teen has and what level of trouble they might get into. Use your instincts, and also your cooking skills! Having lots of snacks and maybe baked goods will feel nurturing to these teens. In addition, if you become a 'cool' parent, then you might find young people come to you with their problems. In my experience, transparency about your boundaries (like no drugs and if you come in with drugs you will have to inform their parents) is helpful and most teens will respect you for it.

▶ **'Keeping you in mind' gestures like a shared journal or thoughtful cards.** The idea of 'keeping the teen in mind' is providing symbolic objects which represent the care and love you have for them. If your teen pushes you away and you just cannot manage to sit down and talk to them, find alternative ways of communicating. Buy a journal and write back and forth with your teen. This way, you can send them a message which they can hold onto and think about without the pressure of being in your presence. Or buy some little note cards and write little messages and hide them in their room to discover saying things like 'I am here for you' or 'I love you so much and want to be here for you'. Even though this may not pay off immediately, especially if the teen has attachment issues, it will register and pay off in the end. Texts are also an option, although perhaps less meaningful since they are so accessible and require less effort. Experiment and see what might work for your teen. Sometimes, especially with avoidant or disorganised styles of attachment, young people cannot manage the intimacy of a face-to-face conversation with a parent/carer. Persist.

▶ **Transitional objects.** This is an object (small, symbolic and of little monetary value) that you can give to your teen when they are anxious. For young people with anxious attachment styles or if they are struggling leaving home or going to school, the parent gives a small item which the teen holds in a pocket, bag or as jewellery and it reminds them of you. It is a comfort object as it helps when they are not able to self-soothe. Find an object which is age appropriate and you might be surprised at how effective this is for teens of all ages.

▶ **An 'Honourable Out.'** Be creative and give your teen an 'honourable' exit which saves face when engaging in unhelpful behaviours. We all need to save face, but remind yourself how important peer approval and perception is to most teens. Easy ideas like pulling them aside and having a quiet chat in a natural manner is an obvious idea (one-to-one) and avoiding an authoritarian tone helps. Also, giving them a choice between two options also lessens their sense of disempowerment and shame.

Chapter 18: Key strategies for teachers and other educators

Many of the strategies in the previous chapter may be adaptable to teachers and educators as, in essence, schools become little family hubs that often have more or less healthy family dynamics. Most teachers, teaching assistants, pastoral staff and other educators will express the pulls and pushes they feel with their pupils, some of which are quite personal. We are all humans after all. In a similar manner, the PACE attitude is truly critical and can facilitate and lighten tricky situations that might otherwise turn difficult at times. Strategies might include:

- **Do not take insults personally.** If I had a pound for every insult that was thrown at me over the past 25 years, I would be an exceptionally wealthy woman! If a student calls you a name, consider whether the translation is 'Do I remind him of his mum who is not emotionally present and so when I am nice to him, he does not trust it?'
- **Persist.** Expect resistance as a young person may have emerged from an environment in which their survival strategy was to be an independent 'little adult'. Expect rejection and persist.
- **Be playful, but not 'jokey'.** Playfulness is a magnificent tool as it is gentle, mutual and light. It is very different from humour, which is so often misinterpreted (especially when the student is hypervigilant). By this I mean, imagine if you are very angry with someone. They make a joke. It can diffuse the tension, but it can also be very easily misinterpreted. A young person with a trauma will be on hyper alert mode. This lends itself to misunderstanding because they are seeing everything as a threat and being very self-protective. Please be wary of humour, especially educators! I have seen it time and time again. One day the humour may feel bonding and the next it feels like you set off a bomb in the room and the educator is left feeling puzzled. It is likely you misread the degree of hypervigilance in the room and it has exploded in front of you.
- **Remember that triggers are often invisible.** Often, when a young person 'acts out' in class the trigger is invisible – invisible to you and them! It might be the tick of a clock, it might be sitting far from the exit door, it might be a smell. If they were abused during Halloween time, the smell of wood burning or the sight of a pumpkin might be triggering. Triggers are often sensory and they can be internal to them (like a thought) or external (like a smell or taste). Most teens are not aware of their own triggers and so when you ask, 'Why did you react the way you did?' Their answer, 'I don't know', is not necessarily evasive, but honest. Again, your detective hat is needed.

- **Playfulness is connecting.** Playfulness can be self-deprecating, though not harsh. Playfulness connects us to our younger selves and equals out the playing field, and can also gently change the power dynamic in the room. I have met many educators or trainers who stay away from playfulness with young people, disregarding it as 'too childish'. This is a mistake. All people like to reconnect with their inner child but we are just too afraid to do it. If you feel unsafe, your child self feels vulnerable and exposed too. This is why using *yourself* as the playful object is key. By this I mean make gentle fun of yourself (e.g., gosh I am so bad at this, I think everyone on the planet is better at Maths than me!). Scoot onto the floor and sit next to them. Surprise them.
- **Find a role model within your school for the adolescent.** Whether it is an older peer or a staff person, there will be someone. This person can be pivotal in meaningful communication and change.
- **Connect with families for help early.** Please reach out, as many parents/carers are overwhelmed by secondary schools and feel estranged as they no longer come to pick up and drop off their child. Also, please do not assume the teen is communicating with their parent/carer, even if you think they have a close relationship. Teens in distress respond best to all adults singing from the same hymn sheet.
- **Be authentic and true to yourself.** As you know from above, young people who are traumatised are hypervigilant and will be extremely attuned to you and your genuineness. Do not pretend to be funny if you are not. Find something you bring to most of your relationships and bring it to the table, so to speak. Here, examples might help.

  If you know you have a good sense of humour with your friends, you can probably joke around (making fun of yourself or situations, not of the young person directly). If you are not, perhaps you are a 'caregiver' type and connect with your compassion? For example, I am not a particularly funny person, but I know I have a lot of empathy and like to 'take care' of my friends and family. When I work with young people, even if I know they respond to jokes and such, I do not venture down that road. I do what I do best and show my caring side, and we build a therapeutic relationship through this. As much as I have longed to be funny, I am just not. At least not when I am trying. I will, however, be playful. By this, I mean I might make a mistake, own it and then sort of tease myself and say "gosh, I have literally made this mistake about 100 times, when will I ever learn?
- **Self-awareness is key** to the success of your interaction with your student. Throughout this book, we have sought ways to explore ourselves so that we know our limitations and our strengths. I cannot overemphasize the importance of self-awareness, as navigating with traumatised teens can be very triggering and it opens the doors to genuine empathy.
- **Transitional object.** This is an object that the young person can bring from home into school or a special object (given by the attachment person at school) which becomes meaningful for the young person. It becomes a comfort object. The young person carries it around or brings it home (wherever they need extra emotional support) and it symbolically carries the positives of your relationship with them. This can be very useful if the young person suffers from separation anxiety (not wanting to leave home) or is beginning to build a meaningful (mentor-like) relationship at school.

- **Go towards those who push you away.** Now this one is a very difficult. This is a problem many people have, as it is only natural for us to steer away from people who push us away, or at least do not draw us to them. The problem here, though counter-intuitive, is that young people with trauma will often push you away. They might not do it literally (although some might). If a student pushes you away, explore why. Similarly, which students draw you in? Both will inform you about yourself and you probably need to build distance between you and the one you 'like', and build bridges between you and the one you 'dislike'.
- **Boundaries, boundaries, boundaries.** This is a word which is tossed around in a lot of settings. What does it mean? For our purposes, it means how much you share with another person. We may not realize it but we share a lot with a lot of people. Often without thinking through the impact of where this information will land. It can be our 'baggage' but it can also include positive events in our lives. Be mindful that the student will have a different life experience from yours and will assign a different meaning to your story than your own. They may interpret even positive events in a negative light. For example, if you share with your students that you are going away on a weekend break camping with your family, this could stimulate huge envy and hurt. How would an Ellie, Remy, Daisy or most of the young people in our case studies feel?
- **Remember that early trauma lodges itself in our bodies and minds and we may be unaware of it.** In a world of Covid-19 anxiety and lockdowns (during which this book was written), increasing climate change uncertainty, widespread realization of the pervasiveness of exclusion and inequality, and the fight for human rights, those of us who may have carried trauma from before will be re-triggered and its impact on us will be more tenacious than for someone who has not. Often our bodies give us clues as to what is triggering to us, even when we may not know it.
- **An 'Honourable Out'.** Giving struggling teenagers an honourable, non-shameful exit strategy to their unhelpful behaviours in a school setting is probably even more important than in a home setting. Schools are a very public place, in which teens are exposed to the perceptions of their peers, bullying and criticism. Teens are hypervigilant when they are with their peers, even if they look totally relaxed on the surface. I have worked with outwardly robust, street-smart young people who have the same or an even more fragile sense of self-esteem than any other teen. They just mask it better. Please remember to look underneath and do not presume arrogance. Offer them an 'out' which feels like a prideful exit to their unhelpful behaviour. Here, your body language (posture and dominance), tone, facial expression and words will be highly scrutinized and (mis)interpreted. Please deliver reprimands or consequences in private, with a warm and understanding tone. Have a warm and happy face (neutrality can be misinterpreted). Such compassion can begin to build bridges you may not have known existed. We all seek to be 'understood', and you are perfectly positioned to begin to remedy their expectation of shame and lack of understanding.

A final discussion point

In conclusion, I would like to thank you for making this journey with me and as a parting gift, I invite you to think about this quote:

"Those who can stay with, and touch these children, emotionally and psychologically, have the capacity to heal young minds. If relationships are where things developmental can go wrong, then relationships are where they are most likely to be put right." (Howe, 2005)

Chapter 19: Resources

Sexual Assault Survivors

RAINN
www.rainn.org/national-resources-sexual-assault-survivors-and-their-loved-ones

Rape Crisis
https://rapecrisis.org.uk/get-help/

Greatist
https://greatist.com/live/sexual-assault-survivor-resources

Bullying

NSPCC
https://learning.nspcc.org.uk/research-resources/schools/anti-bullying-resources

Respect me resources:
https://respectme.org.uk/resources/

Cyber-bullying

Play:
Evan Placey play: "Girls Like That"

Body image issues

Play:
Anorexia "Hard to Swallow" by Mark Wheeler

Free workbook about BDD:
www.cci.health.wa.gov.au/-/media/CCI/Consumer-Modules/Building-Body-Acceptance/Building-Body-Acceptance---03---Reducing-Appearance-Preoccupation.pdf

Abuse and neglect

A Child called It by Dave Pelzer (a series of three books which was written by a survivor of abuse. As quite brutal, to be shared and discussed, rather than just given to a teen.)

Education strategies for challenging behaviours

https://adelebateseducation.co.uk/miss-i-dont-give-a-sht/
*Miss I don't Give a Sh*t*, by Adele Bates, published by SAGE/Corwin.

Autism Spectrum Condition (ASC)/sensory issues

https://raisingchildren.net.au/autism/learning-about-autism/assessment-diagnosis/signs-of-asd-in-teens

https://myacespace.co.uk/

Suicide

National Suicide Prevention lifeline
800-273-8255/7
Online chat: https://suicidepreventionlifeline.org/chat/ (24/7)

National Institute of Mental health resources
www.nimh.nih.gov/index.shtml

Healthline
www.healthline.com/health/mental-health/suicide-resource-guide

Gender identity issues

NSPCC and NHS have good links to start informing you:

NSPCC
www.nspcc.org.uk/keeping-children-safe/sex-relationships/gender-identity/

NHS
www.nhs.uk/mental-health/conditions/gender-dysphoria/overview/

Young Minds organisation
https://youngminds.org.uk/find-help/for-parents/parents-guide-to-support-a-z/parents-guide-to-support-gender-identity-issues/

Mermaids
https://mermaidsuk.org.uk/

Divorce

www.verywellfamily.com/effects-of-divorce-on-teens-2609530

https://understandingteenagers.com.au/the-impacts-of-divorce-on-teenagers/

Parental suicide

www.healthyplace.com/suicide/for-teens-dealing-with-a-parent-s-suicide

https://afsp.org/story/from-a-child-who-lost-a-parent-to-suicide

Foster care

www.imom.com/teens-in-foster-care/

www.education.ox.ac.uk/wp-content/uploads/2019/05/Teenagers-in-Foster-Care-Handbook-1.pdf

Adoption

https://evolvetreatment.com/blog/adopted-teens-identity-trust/

www.relate.org.uk/relationship-help/help-family-life-and-parenting/parenting-teenagers/family-issues/talking-your-teen-about-adoption

Bereavement

www.cruse.org.uk/get-help/for-parents/teenagers-understanding-of-death

https://whatsyourgrief.com/helping-a-teenager-deal-with-grief-2/

Movies about teen issues

Watching a movie with your teen or you class is a fantastic way to get an issue discussed. I have included 80s and 90s movies as they have had a comeback and are now considered cool by many young people. Please research any of these movies before looking at them as some are quite hard hitting.

Bullying: Breakfast club; Heathers; Welcome to the Dollhouse; Billy Elliott; Mean Girls; Pretty in Pink

Gender Identity issues: Boys don't cry

Body image and self-esteem issues:
My Skinny Sister (anorexia); The Full Monty; Precious

Racism: The Forty-Year-Old Version; Do the Right thing; American History X; Schindler's List; BlacKkKlansman; Get Out; Green Book; Precious

Abuse and Neglect:
Precious; Postcard to Daddy

Grief, Loss and Depression
The Perks of Being a Wallflower; Girl, Interrupted; Virgin Suicides

Bibliography

Ainsworth MD (1978) *Patterns of Attachment: A Psychological Study of the Strange Situation.* New Jersey: Lawrence Erlbaum.

Bowlby J (1969) *Attachment and Loss.* Vol 1, *Attachment,* London: Hogwarth

Crenshaw, Kimberlé (1989) "Demarginalizing the Intersection of Race and Sex: A Black Feminist Critique of Antidiscrimination Doctrine, Feminist Theory and Antiracist Politics". University of Chicago Legal Forum.

Diane Poole Heller (2014) *What's Your Attachment Style* [online]. Available at: https://dianepooleheller.com/attachment-styles/ (accessed January 2022).

Howe D (2005) *Child abuse and neglect: attachment, development and intervention.* London: Palgrave and Macmillan

Hughes D (2017) *Building the Bonds of Attachment: Awakening Love in deeply Traumatized Children,* Rowman & Littlefield Publishers

Klass D, Silverman P & Nickerman S (1996) *Continuing Bonds: New Understandings of Grief* (Death Education, Aging and Health Care), Routledge.

Kübler-Ross E (1969) *On Death and Dying.* Routledge.

Lyubomirsky S & Layous K (2013) *How Do Simple Positive Activities Increase Well-Being?* Volume 22 issue 1, page(s): 57-62, Sage. Online article: https://journals.sagepub.com/doi/abs/10.1177/0963721412469809/

Main M & Solomon J (1986) Discovery of an insecure-disorganized/disoriented attachment pattern: procedures, findings and implications for the classification of behaviour', in T.B.. Brazelton and MW Yogman (eds) *Affective development in Infancy.* New Jersey: Norwood.

Music G (2017) *Nurturing Natures: Attachment and Children's Emotional, Sociocultural and Brain Development.* Routledge.

Moll J et al (2006) Human-fronto-mesolimbic networks guide decisions about charitable donations. *Proceedings of the National Academy of Sciences.*

Siegel DJ (1999) *The developing mind: How relationships and the brain interact to shape who we are.* New York; Guilford Press.

Thomas SA NBC article by Nicole Spector, May 19, 2019. *Working while mourning: how to grieve when you're on the job* [online]. Available at: www.nbcnews.com/better/lifestyle/working-while-mourning-how-grieve-when-you-re-job-ncna995946

Winnicott D (1953) Transitional Objects and Transitional Phenomena, *International Journal of Psychoanalysis*

Acknowledgments and thank yous

Most of all, I would like to thank all the teens I work with in my present private work, but also Homewood College, my old special school in Brighton and Hove. Thank you for letting me enter your worlds. You were, and continue to be, my muses!

Thank you to the Homewood staff and all my ACE colleagues who gave me 15 years of invaluable support, tales to remember and a feeling of being valued as a team member.

To name just a few (and I am sorry for those I have missed out – it has been over 15 years; it does not mean I don't thank you and deeply appreciate you):

Martin B who is so fair minded, with an enormous heart and common sense and was my sidekick and is my true friend;

Rachel and your endless perseverance and passion for kids;

the indominable Katie whose energy and positivity fills you up;

Ewan whose heart is so big and sensitive;

Rob who is gentle and actually funny;

both Jos (you know who you are) with your dedication to the core;

Lucy whose heart is unbridled and earnest;

Tino whose faith and hard work is always a comfort to all;

Lynne who is the eternal school mama;

James who always wants to dream bigger;

both Lisa Ss who are so deeply committed to the kids;

Mark H and Anthony who were a dynamic duo;

La belle Helene who was and is a wonder woman;

Craig N who is just such a kind and compassionate leader;

Karen M who is my sensory guru and whose kindness is ever-present; and

Adele who was my role model in writing this book.

Finally, Chris Walsh who welcomed me to the ACE world with your peaceful presence well over 15 years ago, and what a journey that was!

Deep thanks also to:

Darren Reed (and your team), from Pavilion Publishing, whose gentle and steady approach and suggestions only added to both the quality of the book and my experience as a first-time author; a true gift.

Nikka (but Nikki to me) whose spirit, sense of exploration and deep talent, only encourages me to keep on going!

Jo R whose support, laughter and clarity of thought has always accompanied me.

Jamie Carter, the type of paediatrician who actually cares and is a model to me.

Graham Music who is just the type of therapist and author I would dream to be.

Deborah (bb) who is always by my side and helped me so much when thinking about this book during our adventurous sea swims and whose challenge, support and deep friendship is always a treasure to me.

Michelle Ma Belle who inspires me always, as a deep and loving woman, true friend and dedicated mother.

Jess whose profundity of spirit and patience always touch and support me.

Liz whose life enthusiasm, energy and verve surpass my own!

Lucy whose gentle questions and true generosity always provoke deeper thought and a belief in yourself.

Geraldine (Gigi) who is my model of genuine non-judgemental compassion.

Cathy whose gentleness cradles you.

My Bookettes, my dear friends, Nicole, Sharon, Lucy, Deborah and Fiona (in spirit) whose attempts to write books that are yet to come to fruition, helped fuel me to write this one.

Loretta, who knows me too well and whose care, support and persistence got me to publish this book!

Valerie Moss whose tenderness has always made me smile.

Ivan whose love for language touches me and everything you do.

Isabelle and Hubert, whose long friendship with me and our family always steadies me and fills me with past (and future) moments of joy.

Candice whose faith in me and my eternal optimism has always been at my side since childhood.

Violy who is just such an inspiration in her own life story and her generosity of spirit touches me and everyone around her.

Laura whose brightness and deep caring, both in terms of intelligence and in behaviour, is always so supportive of me (and her Oak Park students!).

Damian whose technical genius and incredible patience (with my technical ineptitudes) has helped me out so much in all my freelance ventures.

Ellen whose sensitivity gave me such profound ideas and deep reflections for this book.

Jay who has a gentle and peaceful smile for us all.

Ava who is a little ball of energy and full of creativity (and a teenager herself)!

Mark whose calm and patience is balm to us all.

Jocelyne whose endless warmth and optimism gave me the grounding I needed.

My parents, whose natural enthusiasm, love, support and gentle teasing of my endless energy grounds me.

My sister, Alex, who has always been such a deep thinker and rode my childhood traumas alongside me.

Valerie, my loved mother-in-law, who will always be in my heart and who shared my love of books.

Sovanne and Raph, my hearts, who inspire and teach me every day and fill me with inner love, playfulness and peace; and

Lawrence, who was my first reader, editor and whose belief in and love for me steadies and fuels me always.

Chapter 19: Resources

Photographs and visual acknowledgments

I would also like to thank the photographers, notably:

Raphael Lambrakis-Haddad and model Tommy Taylor (image of "Joe"),

Andrea de Santis (image of "Zoe"),

Brett Sayles (image of "Max"),

Polina Zimmerman (image of "Talia")

"Pasha" (images of "Sam" and "Lili")

Pixabay (images of "Ellie," "Jac," "Zac" and second insecure attachment photo)

Armin Rimoldi (image of "Tyree")

Anna Schvets (image of "Jazz")

Inzmam Khan (image of "Saul")

Sofia Alejandro (image of "Daisy')

Daniel Reche (image of "Remy")

Nhan Duong (image of "Sasha")

Deden Ricky Ramdhani (image of grief)

Kelvin Octa and Mervyert Gonullu (images of attachment styles)

"Nappy" (image of secure attachment)

Саша Лазарев, Pixabay and Alexander Krivitskiy (images of insecure attachment)

Thank you to Pexels.com, a brilliant website which features amateur and other photographers, from which most of the images above were taken.

Thank you to Diane Poole Heller and her generosity in allowing me to use her Attachment Styles quiz in this book.